MW01488167

LATIN COMPOSITION

AN ELEMENTARY GUIDE

TO

WRITING IN LATIN

PART I. — CONSTRUCTIONS

BY

J. H. ALLEN AND J. B. GREENOUGH

Adam C Moore
1 September 2011
Woodway, Texas, USA

BOSTON

GINN BROTHERS

1875

Cambridge :
Press of John Wilson and Son.

PREFACE.

THIS book completes the series of preparatory text-books announced by the present editors. It has been prepared with a view to furnish a sufficient amount of study and practice in Latin composition, during the last year of preparation for college, or the first of a college course. It supposes in the learner a fair acquaintance with the language, gained by the reading of the usual authors and the careful study of grammar and notes, with some elementary practice in writing, at least as much as that given in the " Method," to which this is intended as a sequel.

" Latin Composition," so called, has often been taught solely by the use of detached sentences illustrating the various constructions of syntax, translated out of Roman authors, to be re-translated into the original form. We are persuaded that, however serviceable this may be to give a certain mechanical familiarity with the formal rules of Grammar, it is not a good preparation for " composition," in the sense that properly belongs to that word. The best way to learn intelligently the usages of the language is to put *real English into real Latin*. While we seek, therefore, to cover the entire ground of syntactical constructions, the suggestions given in this book are throughout from the English point of view. The question we have attempted to answer is not "How closely may this or that phrase in Cicero be imitated by the learner?"

but, "How may good common English be best represented in Latin forms?" We would thus suggest a comparison not merely of the words or the constructions, but (so to speak) of the genius and spirit of the two tongues, which, we are convinced, is the true way of appreciating what is most characteristic and best worth knowing in the ancient authors.

With this view, the passages to be rendered into Latin are freely selected from the sources which seemed suitable to our purpose.* It will be observed that we have very early introduced continuous paragraphs or narratives ; which, we believe, are not only more interesting in themselves, but will be found easier in practice than detached sentences, besides the advantage of exhibiting the rarer constructions *in situ,* and not as mere isolated puzzles. The extracts have been very carefully selected, with a view not to anticipate constructions not already given ; or, where this is inevitable, it is hoped they are sufficiently helped by notes and vocabulary, while they are accompanied in every case by full preliminary instruction.†

The earlier of these extracts are chiefly anecdotes from Roman history, or other matter within a range already familiar to the pupil. In the later ones we have been obliged to introduce, here and there, modern material and ideas. These, it is likely, will tax more severely the pupil's knowledge and capacity ; but it seems evident that the more intricate constructions of Latin prose can be best understood when we meet them from our own point of view, and find the need of them to express our own forms of thought. It should be understood that the difficulties they include are *those of the language itself;* and it is best to meet them fairly at the start, rather than evade or disguise them. There is no such thing

* Of these we may specify Smith's "Smaller History of Rome," and Sargent's "Easy Passages for Translation into Latin."

† It may be worth while to suggest that the teacher may at his pleasure select single passages or phrases for elementary practice.

as making a Ciceronian period or an indirect discourse in
Cæsar or Livy an easy thing to boys ; and the student is not
fairly master of them until he can to some extent follow and
reproduce them in his own work.   The difficulties may, however, be lightened to any extent, at the discretion of the
teacher, even to the extent of going over in detail the whole
ground of each exercise in advance.

CAMBRIDGE, July 10, 1875.

ERRATA.

LATIN COMPOSITION.

Page 12, line 5 from bottom, read *laudis*.

   ,,   17, ,, 14 ,,   ,,   ,,   § 21.

   ,,   26, ,, 12 ,,   ,,   ,,   Lesson 17.

   ,,   56, ,,   4 ,,   ,,   ,,   with pres. ind. (or subj.).

   ,,   93, ,, 21 for *conjurator* ,, *conjuratus, i.*

CONTENTS.

PART. I. — CONSTRUCTIONS.

COMPOSITION.

PART FIRST. — CONSTRUCTIONS.

Lesson 1.

The Order of Words.

READ carefully the whole of § **76.** Learn subsection 1, with *c, d ;* and 2.

NOTE. — Though the order of words in a Latin sentence seems very arbitrary, yet it will be observed that almost every arrangement produces some effect such as must usually be given in English by emphasis or stress of voice. In the Exercises to follow, the pupil should observe the reason of any change he may make from the normal order, and the effect it has in making prominent some particular word or words. He should also acquire, as early as possible, the habit of regarding his composition *as a Latin sentence*, and not *as an English sentence turned into Latin words.* And he will be aided in this by habitually reading over the sentence *as Latin* after he has written it, to be sure that it has a Latin sound.

1. The normal or regular form of words in a Latin sentence is the following : (*a*) The Subject, followed by its modifiers ; (*b*) the modifiers of the Predicate, the *direct object* being usually put last ; (*c*) the Verb, preceded by any word or phrase which directly qualifies its action.

This is the order usually to be followed, where no emphasis is thrown on any particular word, as in simple narrative of fact : thus,

Hannibal imperator factus | proximo triennio omnes gentes Hispaniae | bello subegit. — NEPOS, Hann. 3.

REMARK. — In actual practice, the normal order of words is rarely found. It is continually altered, either for the sake of *emphasis*, — to throw stress on the more important words ; or for the sake of *euphony*, — to make the sentence more agreeable to the ear.

2. Modifiers of Nouns — as adjectives (not predicate), appositives, and oblique cases used as attributes — usually follow the noun ; modifiers of Verbs — including adverbs and adverbial phrases — precede the verb. Genitives may come indifferently before or after the noun which they limit.

3. In the arrangement of Clauses, the *relative clause* regularly comes first in Latin, and usually contains the antecedent noun ; while, in English, the *demonstrative clause* almost always precedes : as,

Quos amisimus cives, eos Martis vis perculit. — Cic. Marc. 6. ("Those citizens whom," &c. See examples in § 48, 3. *b.*)

4. In contrasted phrases or clauses, either (1) the same order of words is repeated (*anaphora*), or (2) the order is reversed (*chiasmus*) : as,

1. *Bellum genere necessarium magnitudine periculosum.* — id. Manil. 10.
2. *Non terrore belli, sed consilii celeritate.* — (id. 11.)

5. Almost universally the MAIN WORD of the sentence is put first. This main word may be (1) simply the emphatic word, containing the idea most prominent in the writer's mind (*emphasis*) ; or it may be (2) contrasted with some other word preceding or following (*antithesis*). Compare, for example, the following : —

1. *M. Brutus Ciceronis amicus Caesarem interfecit.*
2. *Amicus Ciceronis M. Brutus Caesarem interfecit.*
3. *Caesarem interfecit M. Brutus Ciceronis amicus.*

That is, "It was Cæsar," &c.

4. *Interfecit Caesarem M. Brutus Ciceronis amicus.*

Here the emphasis is thrown on the *fact* of killing : compare —

5. *Interfectus est propter quasdam seditionum suspi-tiones C. Gracchus.* — Cic. Cat. i. 2 (see the passage).

6. *Romae summum otium est.*

Here Rome is contrasted with Syria, which Cicero had just spoken of.

Lesson 2.

Rules of Agreement. — 1. Apposition.

REVIEW § **46**, 1, 2 ; Learn *a, b, c.*

Observe that in Latin simple apposition is often used where in English we use *as, of, when,* or even a separate clause : thus,

1. To act as a mother, *matrem se gerere.*
2. To treat Cicero as a friend, *Cicerone amico uti.*
3. To regard the gods as immortal, *deos aeternos habere.*
4. The city of Rome, *Roma urbs.*
5. I remember seeing when a boy, *puer memini videre.*
6. Publius and Lucius Scipio, *P. et L. Scipiones.*
7. Cato used to tell in his old age, *Cato senex narrabat.*
8. Fabius in his second consulship (when he was second time consul), *Fabius consul iterum.*

N.B. In the following Exercises, words in brackets are to be omitted in the Latin.

Proper Names of the first or second declension are not given in the Vocabulary, except where the spelling is different in English.

Exercise 1.

1. The consul Caius Flaminius defeated the Insu-brians.[1] The next consuls, Scipio and Marcellus, con-

---

[1] Prænomens (as Caius) are always to be abbreviated (see § **15**, 4). The name must here precede the title (see Note on page 1).

tinued the war. Marcellus slew Viridomarus, chief of the Insubrians, and Scipio his colleague took Milan, their chief town. 2. Give this message[1] to Tarquinius, your king. 3. O father Tiber, take me [into thy charge] and bear me up. 4. We have sworn together, three hundred noble youths, against Porsena. 5. Bocchus was gained over to the Roman cause by Sulla, the quæstor of Marius. 6. The consul Publius Rupilius brought the ᛁServile War to an end by the capture of Tauromenium and Enna, the two strongholds of the insurgents. 7. Sempronia, the only sister of Tiberius Gracchus, was married to the younger Scipio Africanus. 8. The next year, Lucius Cornelius Scipio, brother of the great Africanus, and Caius Lælius, the intimate-friend of the latter,[2] were consuls. 9. The Illyrians were a nation of pirates. 10 The she-wolf acted [as a] mother. 11. The Academy introduced a new [branch of] knowledge [viz.] to know nothing. 12. Demetrius, an unprincipled Greek, surrendered to the Romans the important island [of] Corcyra. 13. Marius and Cicero were born at Arpinum, a free-town of Latium.

[1] Literally, " Report these [things]."   [2] *idem.*

Lesson 3.

Rules of Agreement. — 2. The Verb.

1. REVIEW § **49** (the general rule of agreement). Learn the sub-sections 1 with *a, b;* 2. *a, b.*

NOTE. — The correspondence of the verb with its subject (called agreement) is nearly the same in most languages, though obscured in English by the loss of the inflectional endings. The peculiarities of Latin use are given in the sub-sections cited above. The most important of these is the regular omission of the personal pronoun of the first or second person as subject (the pronoun being contained in the verb-ending [1]), also of the third person whenever it is plain from the context. Hence the rule —

2. The personal pronoun is never to be expressed in Latin, except when required for emphasis or precision.

3. A single idea is very often expressed in Latin by two nouns connected by a conjunction (*hendiadys*). In this case the singular verb is the usual form : as,

There is a continued series of events, *est continuatio et series rerum.*

4. The following examples show the most frequent Latin usages : —

1. **Fannius and Mucius came to their father-in-law,** *Fannius et Mucius ad socerum venerunt.*
2. **Neither Ælius nor Coruncanius thought so,** *nec Aelius nec Coruncanius ita putabat.*
3. **Balbus and I held up our hands,** *ego et Balbus sustulimus manus.*
4. **If you and Tullia are well, Cicero and I are well,** *si tu et Tullia valetis, ego et Cicero valemus.*
5. **Water and earth remained,** *aqua restabat et terra* (more rarely : *aqua et terra restabat*).
6. **I say,** *aio ;* **they say (people say),** *aiunt.*
7. **I strongly approve of Epicurus, for he says, &c.,** *Epicurum valde probo, dicit enim, etc.*
8. **Rational instruction prescribes,** *ratio et doctrina praescribit.*

N.B. The periphrastic forms of the verb come properly under the treatment of Adjectives, and are included in the next Lesson.

---

[1] So sometimes in old English or in poetry : as, *Did'st ever see the like ?* (Taming of the Shrew, iv. 1). So the phrases, *thank you, pray come,* &c.

Exercise 2.

1. Catulus in the Senate, and Cato in the forum, hailed Cicero [as] the father of his country. 2. Cicero calls Athens the inventress of arts. 3. The army of Hannibal lived luxuriously at Capua, a beautiful city of Campania.[1] 4. We avoid death as-if a dissolution of nature. 5. Many ancient peoples worshipped the dog and cat [as] gods. 6. The swallow, harbinger of Spring, had now appeared. 7. Marcus Manlius, the preserver of the capitol, came forward [as] the patron of the poor. 8. The censors, Crassus and Mænius, created two new tribes, the Ufentine and Falerian. 9. Quintus and I[2] shall set sail to-morrow; you and Tiro will wait [for] us in the harbor. 10. Honor and shame from no condition rise. 11. To you, [my] son Marcus, belongs the inheritance of my glory and the imitation of my deeds. 12. Never is danger overcome without danger, as they say. 13. The exigency[3] of the occasion[3] demands severity. 14. The mad-scheme of Saturninus and the discredit of Marius gave-new-strength[4] to the Senate.

[1] See § **46**, 2. *b*   [2] In Latin, "I and Quintus."
[3] Two words with *et.*   [4] *Confirmo.*

Lesson 4.

Rules of Agreement.—3. Adjectives.

1. LEARN § **47** (the general rule of agreement); also sub-sections 1 and 2, with *a*, *b*.

NOTE. — As adjectives are not inflected at all in English, the beginner is required to pay constant attention to the rule. The only special difficulties likely to arise are when the same adjective belongs to two nouns, especially when these are of different genders. As to these, the principles stated in 2, with *a* and *b*, will in general be a sufficient guide.

2. The participial forms in the compound tenses, as well as other participles, are treated in construction as adjectives : as,

1. Cæsar and Bibulus were elected consuls, *Caesar et Bibulus consules creati sunt.*
2. Tullia is dead (or died), *Tullia mortua est.*
3. Both consuls were slain, *uterque consul occisus est.*
4. Virginius and his daughter were left alone before the judgment-seat, *Virginius et filia ejus soli ante tribunal relicti sunt.*
5. The wife and little son of Regulus embraced him as he departed, *Regulum discedentem uxor et parvus filius amplexi sunt.*

Exercise 3.

1. Brutus, the deliverer of his country, and Collatinus the husband of Lucretia, were chosen first consuls at Rome. 2. Disunion and distrust were created among the allies by the Julian law. 3. Herculaneum and Pompeii [1] have been preserved to our times. 4. The entire Senate and Roman people went out to meet [2] Cicero on his return from exile. 5. All sensible [people] had become alarmed at the mad-conduct of Saturninus. 6. Valerius commanding the foot, and Brutus being appointed to head the cavalry, went out to meet Tarquin on the Roman borders. 7. My uncle and myself, having returned to Misenum, passed an anxious and doubtful night. 8. Manlius during-his-absence [3] had been elected consul a second time. 9. Pompey, having marched into Syria, deposed Antiochus, and made the country a Roman province. 10. The conspiracy against Caesar's life was set-on-foot by Caius Cassius Longinus, an enemy [of] his.

[1] Supply *urbes* in apposition.
[2] *Obviam* with dative, following *egredi.*   [3] *absens.*

11. Mantua, alas! too near unhappy Cremona.[1]
12. You have before your eyes Catiline, the most audacious of men. 13. Aurora opens the purple doors and the courts full of roses. 14. A boar is often held by a small[2] dog. 15. The wall was common to[3] both houses, and was cleft by[4] a narrow chink. 16. Lepidus was defeated near the Mulvian bridge by Catulus, and sailed with the remainder of his forces to Sardinia.

[1] Dative.   [2] *non magnus.*   [3] Genitive.   [4] Ablative.

Lesson 5.

Adjectives: Special Uses.

1. REVIEW § **47.** Learn 3, 4 (adjectives used as nouns), with 6, 8, 9.

Under these heads occur many common phrases, in which the Latin usage must be carefully distinguished from the English: as,

1. I saw Scipio in his lifetime, *Scipionem vivum vidi.*
2. He came against his will, *invitus venit.*
3. Every thing was safe, *omnia tuta erant.*
4. All of us are here, *omnes adsumus.*
5. He was the first to see (he saw first), *primus vidit.*
6. On the top of a tree, *in summa arbore.*
7. The inner part of the house, *interior domus.*
8. The rest of the crowd remained, *reliqua multitudo manebat.*

NOTE. — The use of adjectives as nouns is most common in the masculine plural, just as in English *the wise, the brave,* &c. In the singular this use is rare, except with a few words which have become practically nouns, such as **familiaris,** *an intimate friend;* **sapiens,** *a wise man;* **avarus,** *a miser,* and with neuters as in 4. *a.* In other cases the noun is generally expressed; and almost always when a feminine or neuter would be used. Hence —

2. When any ambiguity would arise from the use of the adjective alone, a noun must be added : as,

1. **Boni,** *the good ;* omnia, *every thing.*
2. **All [men] must die,** *omnibus moriendum est.* But —
3. **A good man,** *vir bonus.*
4. **Power over every thing,** *potentia omnium rerum.*

3. When any other case is used than the nominative or accusative, the noun is more commonly expressed, even when not required for distinctness.

4. An abstract notion is very often expressed in Latin by an adjective in the neuter plural : thus,

1. **All men praise bravery,** *omnes fortia laudant.*
2. **The past at least is secure,** *praeterita saltem tuta sunt.*
3. **Choose the better part,** *elige meliora.*
4. **Fleeting good,** *bona caduca.*
5. **Pleasing ill,** *mala blanda.*

5. Adjectives are often used in Latin where in English we use the possessive, or a noun and preposition : as,

1. **The fight at Cannae,** *pugna Cannensis.*
2. **Caius Blossius of Cumae,** *C. Blossius Cumanus.*
3. **Another man's house,** *aliena domus.*

NOTE. — These adjectives most commonly represent the genitive, and will be treated in Lesson 15, *b.*

Exercise 4.

1. Duillius was-the-first [1] of the Romans to [1] conquer in a naval battle ; Curius Dentatus first led elephants in a triumph. 2. Right and wrong are by nature opposed to-each-other.[2] 3. After [his] exile Scipio passed the-rest-of his life at Liternum, a small town of Latium. 4. Demosthenes, the Athenian orator, being banished from his country on [3] a false charge

[1] Simple adjective.   [2] *Inter se.*   [3] *Ob.*

of having received money[1] from Harpalus, was-in-exile at Megara.[2] He [was] afterwards recalled [and] returned [to] Athens in a ship sent for that [purpose]. 5. Octavia and Livia, the one the sister of Augustus, the other [his] wife, had lost [their] sons, the[3] [famous] young Marcellus and Drusus Germanicus. 6. The aged senators who-had-been-consuls[4] or censors[4] sat in the Forum on [their] curule chairs, awaiting death. The Gauls found the city deserted; but marching on they came to the Forum, where they beheld the old men sitting immovable like beings[5] of[6] another[6] world.[6] For some time they stood[7] in-awe-at[8] the strange sight, till one of the Gauls ventured to go up to Marcus Papirius and stroke his white beard. The old man smote him on the head with[9] [his] ivory staff; then the barbarian slew him, and all the rest were massacred.

[1] Lit. "of money received."   [2] Abl. plural.   [3] *ille.*
[4] Adjectives.   [5] *forma ac natura.*   [6] *de caelo delapsus.*
[7] *Obstipesco.*   [8] *admirans* followed by acc.   [9] Ablative.

Lesson 6.

Pronouns. — 1. Personal and Reflexive.

1. REVIEW § **19** (Personal and Reflexive Pronouns) ; with 3. *a* (Possessive adjectives), *d*, *e*. Observe that the pronouns have almost precisely the same syntax as nouns.

2. The Latin never uses the plural of the second person (**vos**) for the singular *you;* but often the plural of the first person (**nos**) for the singular *I.*

3. Of the double forms in the genitive plural, the form in **um** is partitive, while that in **i** is objective : thus,

1. The elder of us, *major nostrum.*
2. Mindful of us, *memor nostri.*

4. The Reflexive pronoun (**se**), with its corresponding Possessive (**suus**), is used in some part of the *predicate*, always referring to the subject of the sentence or clause.

NOTE. — In such cases we generally (not always) use *self, selves*, and *own*. These accordingly are not necessary in Latin, — except when they are emphatic, — being expressed by the reflexive or the personal pronoun (**me, te**, &c.) : —

1. **Virtue knows itself,** *Virtus se novit.*
2. **Brutus slew his friend,** *Brutus amicum* [*suum*] *occidit* (**his own friend,** *suum amicum*).
3. **Philosophy has much pleasure in it,** *Philosophia multum habet in se delectationis.*

5. The Possessives (like other adjectives) take the gender, number, and case of the noun they are used with, not of the one they refer to. They are regularly omitted when they are plainly implied in the context.

Exercise 5.

1. Bulls defend themselves by [their] horns, boars by their tusks,[1] [and] lions by their teeth and claws. 2. Horatius slew his sister with his own hand. 3. "Young man," said Sulla, "you have strengthened your rival against yourself." 4. "Varus, Varus," cried Augustus, "give me [2] back my legions." 5. Crassus, indeed, has defeated the enemy ; but I have exterminated them root-and-branch. 6. "Who art thou," said Brutus, "and for what purpose art-thou-come ?"[3] "I am thy evil genius,[4] Brutus," replied the spectre ; "thou shalt see me to-morrow at Philippi." 7. Cicero was accustomed to write down his orations. 8. Few men know their own faults and vices. 9. How long a letter I have written to you with my own hand !

[1] *ictus dentium.*   [2] Dative.   [3] Perfect active.   [4] *Furia.*

10. Ancus Martius instituted the college of Heralds; he also founded a colony at Ostia, at the mouth of the Tiber, and built a fortress on the Janiculum.   11. Very agreeable to me is your remembrance of me (plur.).

Lesson 7.

Pronouns. — 2. Demonstrative.

1. REVIEW § **20**, and learn carefully the sub-sections 2. *a* to *e* (use of the Demonstratives).

NOTE. — These Demonstratives are used much like the corresponding words in English, *this, that,* &c.   Observe, however, that though they run into one another in meaning, yet regularly **hic, ille, iste,** are true demonstratives, and actually point to something : while **is** (the pronoun of reference) only refers without pointing out.   Thus *a, a man, the man, one* (*who*), &c., are often rendered by **is** with **qui** following.

2. The Possessives *his, hers, its, theirs,* are expressed by the genitive of a demonstrative, and have no difference of gender in the singular.

3. When the word *that* is used instead of repeating a word before expressed, it is regularly omitted in Latin.   But when *a distinct object* is referred to, it may be expressed by **ille, hic,** or even **is**; or the noun itself may be repeated.   Thus, —

1. I prefer the art of memory to that of forgetfulness, *memoriae artem quam oblivionis malo.*
2. Virtue seeks no other reward except this [of which I have just spoken] of glory, *nullam virtus aliam mercedem desiderat praeter hanc ╷audis.* — CIC. Arch. 11.

NOTE. — In such cases, the Latin often prefers some possessive adjective or other construction (see hereafter, Lesson 15) : as,

The army of Cæsar defeated that of Pompey at Pharsalus, *Caesaris exercitus Pompeianos ad Pharsalum vicit.*

4. Contrary to the English usage, **hic** is generally used to refer to a preceding statement or example; **ille** to a following one: as,

That [which I have just mentioned] is a great argument, but this is a greater: [namely] that, etc., *hoc magnum est argumentum, sed illud majus, quod, etc.*

5. **Hic** often corresponds with our *here, the present;* **ille** to our *there;* and **iste**, *yonder* (*by you*): as,

1. Caius Cæsar here, *hic C. Caesar.*
2. Those benches yonder (by you), *ista subsellia.*
3. The present (now living) Mucius Soævola, *hic Mucius Scaovola.*

6. The demonstrative pronoun regularly agrees in gender and number with a predicate appositive if there is one: as,

This is the toil, this the task, *hic labor hoc opus est.*

7. The intensive **ipse** is usually put in the case of the subject, even where the real emphasis appears to be on the object: as,

1. You praise yourself over much, *ipse te nimium laudas.*
2. This thing is sufficient in itself, *haec res per se ipsa satis est.*

N.B. — The distinction between the intensive **ipse** and the reflexive **se** — both rendered in English by "*self*" — requires to be carefully observed (see § **20**, 2. *e*, N.). **Ipse** often expresses *even, very,* or *just:* as,

1. This very thing, *hoc ipsum.*
2. It is just three years, *tres anni ipsi sunt.*

Exercise 6.

1. Æneas carried with him into Italy his son Ascanius and the sacred Penates of-Troy.[1] He was kindly received by Latinus, king of the country, and married

---

[1] Adjective.

his daughter Lavinia. 2. All philosophers, and among them Epictetus, were banished from Rome by Domitian. 3. The ancients regard this [as] true riches, this [as] a good reputation and great renown. 4. While [1] all arrogance is hateful, at-the-same-time [1] that of genius and eloquence is by-far the most offensive. 5. Diseases of the mind are more dangerous than those of the body. 6. The self-same Cato, the Censor, thus discourses in that very book of Cicero on Old Age. 7. When I listen-to Cicero, I desire to write down his orations, so greatly they delight me. 8. Romulus killed with his own hand Acron, king of Cænina, and dedicated his arms to Jupiter. 9. Upon [2] the death of Numa an interregnum again followed; but soon after Tullus Hostilius was elected king. His reign was as warlike as that of Numa had been peaceful. 10. Servius, the sixth king of Rome, gave his two daughters in marriage to the two sons of Tarquinius Priscus, Lucius and Aruns. The former was proud and haughty; the latter, unambitious and quiet. 11. This was the third and last attempt [on the part] of the Tarquinii; for by this victory the Latins were completely humbled, and Tarquinius Superbus could apply to no other state for assistance. He had already survived all his family, [3] and he now fled to-Cumæ, [4] where he died a wretched and childless old man.

[1] *cum ... tum.*   [2] Ablative.   [3] Dative.   [4] Accusative.

Lesson 8.

Pronouns. — 3. Relative.

1. REVIEW § **48** (rule of Agreement), reading carefully the Note; together with sub-sections, 1, 2, 4.

NOTE. — A relative word used as in English, merely to introduce a descriptive fact, is as simple in construction as a demonstrative, and requires no special rule. Several classes of relative clauses in which the mood of the verb is affected (see § **69**, 2) will be treated hereafter.

N.B. — Relative words include relative Pronouns, Adjectives, and Adverbs; with the indefinites **quisquis** and **quicumque**, *whoever*.

2. The relative is never to be omitted in Latin, though it often is in English. Thus, —

1. The book you gave me, *liber quem mihi dedisti.*
2. I am the man I always was, *is sum qui semper fui.*
3. He is in the place I told you of, *eo in loco est de quo tibi locutus sum.*

3. The relative is often used in Latin where other constructions are used in English; particularly where we should use a participle, appositive, or noun of agency: as,

1. The book entitled Brutus, *liber qui dicitur Brutus.*
2. The existing laws, *leges quae nunc sunt.*
3. The men of our day, *homines qui nunc sunt.*
4. Cæsar the conqueror of Gaul, *Caesar qui Galliam vicit.*
5. True glory the fruit of virtue, *justa gloria qui est fructus virtutis.*

4. In formal or emphatic discourse, it is often better to place the relative clause first; and in such cases it usually contains the antecedent noun: as,

Those evils which we suffer with many seem to us lighter, *quae mala cum multis patimur ea nobis leviora videntur.*

5. When the antecedent noun is in apposition with the main clause or some word in it, it is to be put in the relative clause: as,

Steadfast friends, a class of which there is great lack, *firmi amici, cujus generis est magna penuria.*

6. A relative is constantly used in Latin when English uses a demonstrative with *and* or *but:* as,

1. And since these things are so, *quae cum ita sint.*
2. But if they hesitate or are unwilling, *qui si dubitabunt aut gravabuntur.*

7. When the word AS is used in English as a relative, it must be rendered in Latin by the relative pronoun, adjective, or adverb which corresponds to its demonstrative antecedent: as,

1. The same thing as, *eadem res quae.*
2. Such (men) as, *ei qui.*
3. Such a leader as we know Hannibal to have been, *talis dux qualem Hannibalem novimus.*
4. There were as many opinions as men, *quot homines tot erant sententiae.*

Exercise 7.

1. Tiberius Gracchus was by birth [1] and marriage [2] connected with the noblest families in the Republic: grandson of the conqueror of Hannibal, son-in-law of the chief of the Senate, and brother-in-law of the destroyer [3] of Carthage. 2. Quintus Silo, a Marsian, and Caius Papius Mutilus, a Samnite, who cherished an hereditary hatred against the Romans, were chosen consuls. 3. Sulla with his army was then besieging Nola, a town which was still held by the Samnites. 4. Rome was now exposed to great danger; for those who had been her most faithful friends now rose against her. 5. A day shall come when [4] sacred Troy shall perish. 6. The terms which the general proposed seemed intolerable to the Carthaginians. 7. Tiberius and Caius Gracchus were the sons of Tiberius Sempronius Gracchus, whose measures gave tranquillity

---

[1] *Propinquitas* (plur.).   [2] *Adfinitas* (plur.).
[3] Lit. "of him who destroyed."   [4] Repeat the noun.

to Spain for [1] so many years. They lost their father at [2] an early [3] age. But they were educated with the utmost care by their mother Cornelia, the daughter of Scipio Africanus the elder, who had inherited from [her] father a love [4] of literature, and united[5] in her-person [6] the severe virtue of the Roman matron with a superior knowledge [7] and refinement, which [8] then prevailed [9] in [10] the higher-classes [11] at-Rome.[12] She engaged for [her] sons the most eminent Greek teachers; and from the pains she took [13] with [14] their education they surpassed all the Roman youths of their age.

[1] *per.*	[2] Ablative.	[3] *primus.*
[4] *studium.*	[5] *habeo conjunctam.*	[6] *se.*
[7] *doctrina.*	[8] Neuter plural.	[9] *floreo.*	[10] *apud.*
[11] *nobiles.*	[12] Adjective.	[13] "Take pains," *operam dare.*

[14] Dative.

Lesson 9.

Pronouns: Interrogative and Indefinite.

REVIEW § **22**, 1. with *a* (forms of the Interrogative Pronoun). These forms, including **quisnam**, *who?* (emphatic), and **uter** (see § **16**, 1. *b*), *which of two?* are used much as in English. Thus, —

1. **Who is the man?** *Quis est homo?*
2. **What a man he was!** *Qui homo erat!*
3. **What do you find fault with?** *Quid reprehendis?*
4. **What plan of his do you find fault with?** *Quod consilium ejus reprehendis?*
5. **Which eye aches?** *Uter oculus dolet?*
6. **Which finger hurts?** *Qui digitus dolet?*
7. **Who is it?** (emph.) ⎫
8. **Who in the world (pray who) is it?** ⎬ *Quisnam est? Quis tandem est?*
   (The latter a little stronger.)

2. REVIEW § **21**, 2. *c, d, e, h* (forms and use of the Indefinites).

a. The pronouns which correspond to the English A or SOME, ONE, or ANY (indefinite, not emphatic) are **quis, quispiam, aliquis, quidam.** Of these **quis** is the least definite, and **quidam** the most. When SOME is used of objects *defined in thought* though not named, it is regularly **quidam.** The expressions **nonnullus, nonnemo, nonnihil** are somewhat less definite than **quidam. Quis** is the regular word after **si, nisi, ne, num,** to signify *if any*, &c. With these particles **aliquis** is more definite, like our *if some one*, &c. A FEW or SEVERAL may be expressed by **aliquot, nonnulli, plures; pauci** (restrictive) means *only a few.* The English ANY ONE WHO is often best rendered by **si quis** (See Note, Gr. p. 166).

1. **Some one may say,** *aliquis dicat (dixerit quispiam).*
2. **Some philosophers think so,** *aliqui* (or, if definite persons are thought of, *quidam) philosophi ita putant.*
3. **Some poor women live here,** *habitant hic quaedam mulieres paupercula.* [That is, some women he knows; some women or other would be *aliquae* or *nescio quae.*]
4. **Up runs a man,** *accurrit quidam.*
5. **I will call in a few friends,** *aliquot amicos adhibebo.*
6. **In the very senate-house there is more than one enemy,** *in ipsa curia nonnemo hostis est.*
7. **Banished not on some other charge but this very one,** *expulsus non alio aliquo sed eo ipso crimine.*
8. **He neither denies nor asserts a thing,** *neque negat aliquid neque ait* (**any thing whatever** would be *quidquam*).

b. The pronouns which correspond most nearly with the English ANY (emphatic) are **quisquam** (substantive), **ullus** (adjective), **quivis,** and **quilibet.** The first two are used chiefly with negatives (but see § **21**, 2. *h*) ; the other two are universal (*any you like*). When only two are spoken of, EITHER is **uter** (corresponding to **quisquam**), **utervis, uterlibet** (corresponding to **quivis** and **quilibet**). For the negatives **non quisquam, non ullus, non quidquam, non uter,** use **nemo, nullus, nihil, neuter.**

1. **What can happen to any (one) man can happen to any man (whatever),** *cuivis potest accidere quod cuiquam potest.*

2. **I never did any thing worse,** *numquam quidquam feci pejus.*

3. **Why did I send to anybody before you?** *cur cuiquam misi prius?*

4. **I have less strength than either one of you,** *minus habeo virium quam vestrum utervis.*

5. **No one thinking of any thing but flight,** *nemo ullius rei nisi fugae memor.*

c. The Distributives EACH, EVERY, are expressed by **quisque** (uterque, if there are only two). **Unusquisque** is more emphatic (*every single one*). **Omnis** is sometimes used in the singular in nearly the same sense as **quisque**, but more indefinitely, and is almost equivalent to a plural.

1. **Every good book is better the larger it is,** *bonus liber melior est quisque, quo major.*

2. **Both armies go away every man to his home,** *ambo exercitus suas quisque abeunt domos.*

3. **Each army was in sight of the other,** *uterque utrique erat exercitus in conspectu.*

4. **Every system of instruction** (= all systems of instruction), *omnis ratio et doctrina.*

Exercise 8.

1. Which do you consider the greatest general, Cæsar, Scipio, or Hannibal ? Which the better orator, Cicero or Demosthenes ? 2. "We here bring you war and peace," said the Roman ambassadors in the Senate of the Carthaginians; "which pleases you best ?" 3. Pompey obtained the highest dignity in the State — that of the consulship — without any recommendation of ancestors. 4. The vices of Alcibiades were redeemed by some brilliant qualities. 5. Most men's vices are redeemed by some better qualities. 6. No [1] great man was ever without some divine inspiration. 7. Horace did not read his poetry to any one except friends; and then [2] under compulsion, not everywhere,

---

[1] *nemo.*   [2] Lit. "and that."

nor before[1] everybody [indiscriminately]. 8. Some skill[2] as an orator[3] is necessary to a commander. 9. Several of the allies of Sparta were dissatisfied with the peace she had concluded; and soon after some of them determined to[4] restore the ancient power of Argos. 10. Some slight battles occurred, in which the side[5] of-the-Syracusans[6] had the advantage.[7] 11. Since Agamemnon, no Grecian king had led an army into Asia. 12. It is contrary-to nature to take[8] any thing from any other[9] [person]. Does any one deny this? 13. Whoever had killed a tyrant was praised by the Greeks and Romans. Thus Harmodius, who expelled the sons of Pisistratus, was honored at Athens; Timoleon, who consented-to[10] the death of his brother Timophanes, at Corinth; and Brutus, the slayer of Julius Cæsar, at Rome.

[1] *Coram* with abl. [2] Lit. "Something of skill." [3] Adjective.
[4] Infinitive. [5] *res.* [6] Adjective. [7] Lit. "was superior."
[8] *detraho.* [9] Dative. [10] *probo.*

Lesson 10.

Cases. — 1. As Objects of Verbs.

1. Review §§ **52**, 1. with *a, b* (Accusative as Direct Object); **51**, 1, 2. with *a, b, d* (Dative as Indirect Object); **50**, 4. *a, b, c* (Genitive as the object of verbs of Memory and Feeling); **54**, 6. *d* (Ablative of means, with **utor**, &c.).

2. All of the above cases are used in Latin with different classes of verbs to represent the English Objective case. Thus: —

1. I see the man, *hominem video* (Accusative).
2. I help the man, *homini subvenio* (Dative).
3. I pity the man, *hominis misereor* (Genitive).
4. I treat the man as a friend, *homine amico utor* (Ablative).

REMARK. — In all the above examples the verb is transitive in English, but not really so in Latin. In deciding on the case to be used as the object of any given verb, the following points are to be observed : —

a. The Accusative, as the case of Direct Object, is far more general in its use than either of the others ; and may be assumed to represent the English Objective, except as limited by the special rules which follow.

b. The Dative is to be used, along with the Accusative, wherever in English two object-cases follow, with one of which we may use the preposition TO or FOR (except after verbs of Asking and Teaching, which take two accusatives) : as,

1. He gave me the book (= he gave the book to me), *mihi librum dedit.*
2. I promise you a fig, *tibi ficum promitto.* But —
3. He asked me for money, *pecuniam me rogavit.*
4. Plato taught his scholars geometry, *Plato discipulos suos geometriam docuit.*

The Dative is also to be used after the verbs (apparently transitive) given in the lists in § 51, 2. *a, b, d, e.* These sub-sections, with the accompanying examples and remarks, must be attentively studied ; as an accurate knowledge of these classes of verbs is absolutely essential to the correct use of the language in one of the commonest constructions in Latin.

c. Verbs governing the Genitive in Latin are few, and belong to the strictly limited classes given in the sub-sections under § 50, 4. They are chiefly verbs of Memory and Feeling (with egeo, indigeo, *need*). The genitive of Charge and Penalty corresponds with the English use of the preposition OF.

d. The only verbs governing the Ablative in Latin, corresponding to transitives in English, are the few deponents given in § 54, 6. *d.* Either of them may easily be represented in English by a phrase with a preposition : as,

1. I use (make use of) a sword, *gladio utor.*
2. He eats (feeds on) flesh, *carne vescitur.*
3. They abuse (take advantage of) my friendship, *amicitia mea abutuntur.*

Exercise 9.

1. In our own calamity, we remember the calamities of others.   2. I shall never forget that day : it reminds me at-once [1] of the greatest delight and [1] greatest peril of [2] my life.   3. Pity the sorrows of a poor old man.   4. Bocchus, king of Mauretania, had-pity-on the condition of his son-in-law, Jugurtha, king of Numidia, and promised him aid ; but afterwards, calling-to-mind [3] the greater power of the Romans, betrayed him to Sulla, the quæstor of Caius Marius.   5. The Italians loudly demanded the rights which had been promised them by Drusus.   6. Cæsar forgave all those who had fought on the side of Pompey in the civil war.   7. Marius commanded a separate army in the neighborhood.   8. If a patrician man married a plebeian wife, or a patrician woman a plebeian husband, the State did not recognize the marriage. 9. Dentatus had accompanied the triumphs of nine generals.   As tribune of the people, he most bitterly opposed the patricians.   10. The Knights abused the judicial power, as the Senate had done before. 11. He who commands the sea is lord of affairs.   12. After the Mithridatic war, Pompey, [though] only a private-citizen, performed the part of a commander, levied three legions, and having gained [4] a brilliant victory [4] was received by Sulla with the greatest distinction.   13. Marcus Livius Drusus, like his father, favored the side of the nobles.   But he had promised the Latins and allies the Roman franchise, a measure which had always displeased the Roman people, and which they violently resisted.   Drusus, therefore, had recourse to sedition and conspiracy.   A secret-society

---

[1] *cum ... tum.*   [2] *in.*   [3] *memor*, with gen.   [4] Abl. abs. Pāssive.

was formed, which was bound by oath to obey [1] his commands. The ferment increased, and threatened the safety of the State; but at last Drusus was assassinated in his own house.[2]

[1] *ut pareret.*　　　　　　　　[2] *domi suae.*

Lesson 11.

Cases. — 2. As Modifying Adjectives.

1. REVIEW § **50**, 3. *b, c, d* (Genitive with Adjectives); **51**, 6 (Dative of Fitness, &c.); **54**, 1. *c*, 2. *a*, 3. *a*, 6. *c*, 9. 10. with *a* (various uses of the Ablative).

N. B. These rules include many participles, which are used like adjectives.

2. Adjectives in English almost always require phrases with prepositions when their meaning is to be limited or explained. In Latin this is generally done by using after the adjective the Genitive, Dative, or Ablative case without a preposition.

NOTE. — Some particular adjectives — rather than classes — take a preposition, as in English. These will be treated hereafter, in the Lesson on Prepositions (see § **51**, 6. *a, b*).

a. Relative Adjectives — that is, adjectives whose quality naturally relates to some object, especially one which corresponds to the object of a transitive verb — regularly take the Genitive. This relation is often expressed in English by the preposition OF : as,

1. Mindful of others, forgetful of himself, *memor aliorum oblitus sui.*
2. Disdaining letters, *fastidiosus literarum.*
3. Possessed of reason and judgment, *compos rationis et judicii.*
4. Sharing in the booty, *particeps praedae.*

See also examples under § **50**, 3. *b, c.*

b. Where the relation between the adjective and noun would be expressed in English by the preposition TO or FOR, it is commonly expressed in Latin by the Dative. The chief exceptions are given in § **51**, 6. *a, b, c, d.* (See constructions given in the Vocabulary under each word.)

1. A battle very like a flight, *pugna simillima fugae.*
2. A man hateful to many, *homo odiosus multis.*
3. Times hostile to virtue, *tempora infesta virtuti.*
4. Adjoining the Belgians, *finitimi Belgis.*
5. A law advantageous to the state, *lex utilis rei pub-licae.*

c. When the modifying phrase denotes that *in respect to which* the meaning of the adjective is taken — where the English uses IN, IN REGARD TO, or the like ; sometimes OF — the Ablative is generally used in Latin : as,

1. Lame of one foot, *claudus altero pede.*
2. A man distinguished in war, *vir bello egregius.*
3. Worthy of praise, *dignus laude.*

NOTE. — In this use the Ablative and Genitive approach each other in meaning ; but the Ablative generally expresses a remoter and the Genitive a closer relation. The same relation is often expressed by the Accusative with **ad.**

Exercise 10.

1. Oil rubbed-upon[1] the body makes it more capable of enduring heat, cold, or hardship.   2. Numa instituted a college of priests, four in number.   3. The fifth king of Rome was an Etruscan by birth, but a Greek by descent.   4. The reign of Servius Tullius is almost as barren of military exploits as that of Numa.   5. Wild beasts are not only devoid of reason and speech, but ungovernable[2] in fury, and impatient of control.   6. A Roman patrician had a-number-of[3] clients attached to him, to whom he acted as patron.

---

[1] *inunctus,* with the dative.   [2] *impotens,* with genitive.

[3] *quidam.*

7. Mucius, ignorant of the person [1] of Porsena, killed his secretary instead-of the king himself. 8. Veii was closely allied with Fidenæ. 9. The Pentri inhabited the Apennines. But, not content with their mountain homes,[2] they overran the rich lands of Campania. 10. The season of the year was favorable to Hasdrubal, and the Gauls were-friendly-to his cause. 11. The Roman ambassadors, forgetting their sacred character,[3] fought in the ranks [4] of Clusium. 12. At the beginning of the first Punic war, the Romans had no fleet worthy of the name.[5] 13. Porsena, alarmed for his life, offered terms of peace to the Romans. 14. Cneius Pompey was extremely ambitious of power and glory, and jealous of the superior merit and fame of other men. 15. The Romans were like the Spartans in [6] [their] passion for [7] military glory and empire. 16. The poet Archias, a man endowed with genius and virtue, was regarded by Cicero [as] equal to the most learnèd of the Greeks, and worthy of the highest praise.[8]

[1] *facies.*   [2] *sedes.*   [3] *officium.*   [4] *acies Clusina* (sing.).
[5] *id nomen.*   [6] Ablative.   [7] Genitive.   [8] Plural.

Lesson 12.

Cases. — 3. Indirect Relations.

REVIEW § **51**, 1. 2. with *a, b, d* ; 3. 5. 7 (Dative of Indirect Object, of Possession, of Service, of Reference) ; also § **50**, 4. *d* (**refert** and **interest**).

a. The most common use of TO or FOR in English is represented in Latin by the Dative of Indirect Object : as,

1. The province fell by lot to Cicero, *provincia Ciceroni obtigit.*

2. I consult for the safety of the state, *civitatis saluti consulo.*

3. Medicine is sometimes bad for the health, *medicina valetudini nonnumquam nocet.*

NOTE. — 1. These should be distinguished from the cases where the *direct effect* of an action is spoken of : as,

The dust hurts my eye, *pulvis oculum meum laedit.*

2. The dative of indirect object must also be carefully distinguished from the cases — apparently the same in English — where TO or FOR expresses the *limit of motion.* In Latin all relations of place, *where, whence,* or *whither,* are regularly expressed by means of prepositions (see hereafter, Lesson 15).

b. This construction (dative of indirect object) is used in many cases to express WITH, OVER, UPON, IN, BEFORE, AGAINST, where in the Latin expression a verb compounded with a preposition is used (see list in § **51**, 2. *d :* **ad, ante, con,** &c.) :

1. **A rock hung over his head,** *saxum capiti impendebat.*

2. **I agree with Zeno,** *Zenoni adsentior.*

3. **I set myself against all his plans,** *omnibus ejus consiliis obstiti.*

N. B. — Particular attention must be given to the meaning and construction of each of these compounds in the vocabulary, as many of them are transitive and take the accusative : as,

He besieged the city of Alesia, *urbem Alesiam obsidebat.*

c. The English verb TO HAVE is often, by a Latin idiom, expressed by the Dative with **esse** (compare Note under § **51**, 3) : as,

1. **I have a father at home,** *est mihi pater domi.*

2. **The boy's name is Marcus,** *puero nomen est Marcus* (or *Marco*).

d. The phrases *it belongs to, it is the part of,* and the like, are most commonly expressed in Latin by the Genitive with **esse** : as,

It is the part of wisdom (of a wise man), or, **it is wise,** *est sapientis* (compare *d,* with Remark).

e. TO or FOR is also expressed by the Dative when the object is still more remotely connected with the action, so that the sentence is complete without it (dative of reference) : as,

The good husbandman plants trees for his posterity, *poste-ris suis serit arbores bonus agricola* (compare the examples in § **51,** 7. and *a*).

f. When FOR or OF expresses the purpose or end of an action, the Latin idiom has the dative, often with the dative of indirect object also : as,

1. Cæsar sent three cohorts for a guard, *Caesar tres co-hortes praesidio misit.*

2. It was of great service to our men, *magno usui nostris fuit.*

NOTE. — In English the same relation is often expressed by simple apposition or by the conjunction AS. In Latin this con-struction is limited to a few words, which must be learned by practice (see examples and Remark under § **51,** 5).

g. For the cases in which TO or FOR is expressed by the geni-tive with **refert** and **interest**, see § **50,** 4. *d.* The phrase *for my sake and the republic's* is expressed by **meā et reipublicae causā.**

Exercise 11.

1. The troops of Sulla did no injury to the towns or fields of the Italians. 2. Tiberius Gracchus relied chiefly on the country-people. 3. Both Quintus Ca-tulus and Hortensius were-opponents-of[1] the Gabinian Law. 4. On[2] the arrival of Pompey, Tigranes was obliged to look-to-the-safety-of[3] his own power. 5. The great-numbers[4] of the enemy were a hindrance rather than a help to them. 6. Cæsar's death was undoubtedly a loss not only to the Roman people, but to the whole world. 7. To the modern reader the elegies of Propertius are not so attractive as those of Tibullus. 8. The greatest danger Rome had experi-enced since the time of Hannibal was now impending over the State. 9. The consulship fell to Cneius Octavius, who belonged to the aristocratic-party,[5] and Lucius Cinna, a professed champion of the people.

[1] *obsisto.* [2] Ablative. [3] *prospicio.* [4] *multitudo.* [5] *optimates.*

To their[1] election[2] Sulla made-no-opposition,[3] for it was his own interest to quit Italy immediately. 10. The Gauls once attacked the camp of[4] Quintus Cicero, brother of the orator, [as he was] wintering in Gaul; but Cæsar came to his assistance with two legions, and rescued him. 11. A servant of the consul Opimius, pushing against Gracchus, insolently cried out, " Make way for honest men, you rascals ! " 12. "Stand aside young man," said Cæsar to the tribune Metellus, who vainly attempted to defend the treasury; " it is easier for me to do than say." 13. Damophilus, a wealthy man-of-Enna, had treated his slaves with-excessive-barbarity.[5] They consulted a Syrian slave, whose name was Ennus, who belonged-to[6] another master. This Ennus pretended-to[7] the gift-of-prophecy,[8] and appeared to breathe flames-of-fire. He not only promised them success, but joined in the enterprise himself. 14. " Mother," exclaimed Coriolanus, " thine is the victory, a happy victory for thee, but shame and ruin to thy son."

[1] Relative.   [2] *petitio.*   [3] *non obsistere.*   [4] Dative.
[5] Adverb in superlative.   [6] *servio.*   [7] *sibi adrogare.*
[8] *vis divina.*

Lesson 13.

Cases. —4. Cause, Means, and Quality.

Review § **54,** 4. 6 (ablative of Agent and Means) ; 7. with § **50,** 1. *g* (ablative and genitive of Quality) ; § **54,** 8 with *a* (Price and Value : compare § **50,** 1. *i*) ; also 3 (ablative of Cause), with *a, b, c.*

a. The means, instrument, or agent by which any thing is done we commonly express in English by the preposition by or with. In Latin a distinction is made between the *voluntary agent* (expressed by the ablative with **ab**) ; *a person considered as an* *instrument or means* (expressed by **per** with the accusative); and the *means or instrument* (expressed by the ablative alone, or in special cases by **per** with the accusative). Thus —

1. Cæsar was informed by the ambassadors, *Caesar certior factus est a legatis.*
2. Cæsar was informed by ambassadors (i. e. by means of ambassadors), *Caesar certior factus est per legatos.*
3. Cæsar was informed by letter, *Caesar certior factus est literis* (or *per literas* if the letters were official documents used expressly as means of information).

b. The English ON ACCOUNT OF, FOR, FROM, FOR THE SAKE OF, THROUGH, denoting *cause, occasion,* or *motive,* though oftenest expressed by the ablative alone, are frequently also rendered by prepositions : as,

1. It happened through my fault, *mea culpa accidit.*
2. On account of the pleasure from conversation I delight in entertainments, *propter sermonis delectationem conviviis delector.*
3. We love the good for their virtues, *bonos diligimus propter virtutes* (so *pro meritis*).
4. He could not speak for grief, *loqui prae maerore non potuit.*

So the phrases : — **ex** quo, *on which account;* **ex** eo quod, *for the reason that;* **per** aetatem, *by reason of age;* quam ob rem, *wherefore.* See also Lesson 18.

c. A Quality is very often expressed in English by a noun with the preposition OF : as, *a man of worth, a tale of horror.* In Latin an adjective must be used in such cases, except when the noun of quality has an adjective connected with it, when it may be put either in the genitive or ablative : generally the latter when the noun describes a physical trait. Thus —

1. A man of valor, *vir fortis* (or *fortissimus*).
2. A man of eminent valor, *vir egregiae virtutis.*
3. A man of bodily strength and beauty, *homo validus et pulcher.*
4. Achilles was a man of very great strength and remarkable beauty, *Achilles vir erat summis viribus et eximia pulchritudine.*

d. Manner — in English WITH or IN — is in Latin usually expressed by an Adverb when there is one; otherwise by the ablative, often with **cum** (see § **54,** 7. *b*) : as,

1. **With care,** *accurate* (or, *cum cura*).
2. **In silence,** *tacite* (or, *silentio*).
3. **In the most friendly manner,** *amicissime.*
4. **With the greatest zeal,** *summo studio.*

e. The Price of a thing, — usually given in English with the preposition FOR or AT, — when a *definite sum* is stated, is expressed in Latin by the Ablative ; but *indefinite* price or value is expressed by the Genitives of Quantity (**magni, parvi,** &c.), given in § **54,** 8. *a.* These Genitives often answer to the use of an adverb in English, such as *highly, slightly, not-at-all,* used with expressions of value or esteem. Thus —

1. **How much does this house sell for? ten thousand sesterces.** *Quanti hae aedes veneunt? decies mille nummis.*
2. **I esteem Plato very highly, but the truth more,** *Platonem permagni sed veritatem pluris aestimo.*

Exercise 12.

1. The Veneti had much confidence in their fortified positions. Their coasts were fringed with promontories and peninsulas, and, relying on their strong ships, fully armed and supplied[1] with leathern sails, they were not alarmed even by the greatest tempests of the ocean. 2. A liar[2] hath need of a good memory, but truth is always consistent with itself. 3. I offer myself to thee, O Hercules! because thou art descended from the gods, and givest proofs of that descent by thy love of virtue. 4. Great things are achieved by great exertions, and glory was never the reward of sloth. 5. The Sabines, like most other mountaineers, were brave, hardy, and frugal; and even the Romans looked-up[3] to them [with admiration] on account of their honesty and temperance. 6. Remus leaped in[4]

---

[1] *ornatus.*   [2] Dative.   [3] *admiror.*   [4] *per.*

scorn over his brother's wall. 7. Romulus appeared after [his] death to Proculus in more-than-mortal[1] beauty. 8. Augustus lived with republican simplicity[2] in a plain[3] house on the Palatine [hill], and educated his family with great strictness[4] and frugality.[4] 9. Vitellius was remarkable for his gluttony[5] and his coarse[6] vices. 10. Demosthenes listened awhile to the bland professions of Archias, the actor, but at length replied, "Archias, you never won me by your acting, nor will you now by your promises." 11. Columbus entered the hall surrounded by a brilliant crowd of cavaliers, among whom he was conspicuous for his stately and commanding person.[7] 12. To the English it was a night of[8] hope, fear, suspense, [and] anxiety. They had been wasted by disease, broken with fatigue, and weakened by the many privations which are wont to attend[9] an army marching through a hostile country. But they were supported by the spirit and confidence of their gallant leader, and by the recollection of victories won by their fathers. 13. The forests have given place to cultivated fields, the morass is dried up, the land has become solid, and is covered with habitations. A countless multitude, living in[10] peace and abundance upon the fruits of their labors, has succeeded to the tribes of hunters who were always contending with war and famine. What has produced these wonders? What has renovated the surface of the earth? The name of this beneficent genius[11] is Security.

---

[1] *divinus.* [2] *cultus moderatus* (abl.). [3] *minime sumptuosus.*
[4] Adverbs. [5] *intemperantia gulae.* [6] *turpis.*
[7] *habitus corporis.* [8] *plena.* [9] *esse* [10] *in,* ablative. [11] *dea.*

Lesson 14.

Cases. — 5. Separation and Comparison.

LEARN § **54,** 1. with *a, b, c, d* (ablative of Separation) ; § **51,** 2. *e* (dative with Compounds) ; § **54,** 5. with *a ;* 6. *e* (ablative of Comparison and Degree of Difference).

a. The relations denoted in English by FROM or OF — in such phrases as *to deprive of, to be free from, in want of,* and the like — are in Latin expressed by the ablative : as,

1. He is free from terror, *caret formidine.*
2. To retire from office, *abire magistratu.*
3. A city stripped of defence, *urbs nuda praesidio.*
4. A man without a country, *homo qui caret patria.*
5. You will relieve me of great fear, *magno me metu liberabis.*

N. B. Motion *from a place* is regularly expressed by means of prepositions (see Lesson 17).

b. When a thing is said to be taken away *from a person,* the dative is almost always used instead of the ablative : as,

1. He took a ring from the woman, *mulieri anulum detraxit.*
2. You have robbed me of my property, *bona mihi abstulisti.*

c. The uses of the ablative with the Comparative may be seen in the following : —

1. Nothing is dearer to a man than life, *nihil homini vita est carius.*
2. Quicker than one would think, *opinione celerius.*
3. Much more rich than wise, *multo divitior quam sapientior.*
4. The more dangerous the disease the more praised the physician, *quo periculosior morbus eo laudatior medicus.*
5. The more virtuously one lives, the less he will injure others, *quanto quis vivit honestius tanto minus nocebit aliis.*
6. Not more than two hundred horsemen escaped, *haud amplius ducenti equites effugerunt.*

Exercise 13.

1. The orator Hortensius was eight years older than Cicero. 2. Licinius liberated the plebeians[1] from an oppressive bondage. 3. Rome was now deprived of almost all her allies. 4. The constitution[2] of Lucius Cornelius took from the knights the judicial-power[3] which they had exercised since the times of the Gracchi. 5. Men are much less in bulk than very many animals. 6. Grief and indignation deprived Marius of utterance.[4] 7. Antisthenes, the Cynic, was once very sick,[5] and cried out, "Who will deliver me from these torments?"[6] Then said Diogenes, who by chance was by, "This knife, if you will." "I do not say from my life," he[7] replied, "but from my disease." 8. The archbishop tore the diadem from the head of the statue, and the image, thus despoiled of its honors, was thrown upon the ground. 9. The aged Nestor boasts his virtues, nor seems to be too loquacious; for his speech, says Homer, flowed from his tongue sweeter than honey. 10. Hesiod was robbed of a fair share of his heritage by the unrighteous decision of judges who had been bribed by his brother Perses. The latter was afterwards deprived of his property, and asked relief of[8] his brother. 11. Alcaeus, for instance, cheered by his songs the nobles who had been driven into-exile.[9] 12. After the expulsion of the kings,[10] a new office was created at Rome, called the dictatorship, greater than the consulship. This dignity, however, was discontinued after the second Punic war. The stronger

---

[1] *plebs* (sing.).   [2] *instituta* (plur.).   [3] *judicium.*   [4] *vox.*
[5] *graviter aegrotare.*   [6] *malum.*   [7] *ille.*   [8] *a.*
[9] *e patria* (abl.).   [10] *post reges exactos.*

the Republic became, the less it needed this extraordinary power. But in[1] the civil war it was revived by order of the people, and conferred upon Sulla, who afterwards resigned it and became a private citizen.

[1] Ablative.

Lesson 15.

Cases. — 6. Special Uses of the Genitive.

LEARN § **50**, 2. with Remarks 1. 2. 3 (Partitive genitive) ; 3. *a* (Objective genitive with nouns).

a. When in English one noun is closely connected with another by a preposition, the genitive is commonly used in Latin, no matter what the preposition is in English (objective Genitive : see examples under § **50**, 3. *a*) : as,

1. Prayer to the gods, *precatio deorum.*
2. Escape from danger, *fuga periculi.*
3. Power over every thing, *potestas omnium rerum.*
4. Pain in the head, *dolor capitis.*
5. Confidence in one's strength, *fiducia virium.*
6. Departure from life, *excessus vitae.*
7. Subject for jests, *materia jocorum.*
8. Struggle for office, *contentio honorum.*
9. Relief from duty, *vacatio muneris.*
10. Difference in politics, *rei publicae dissensio.*
11. Reputation for valor, *opinio virtutis.*
12. Union with Cæsar, *conjunctio Caesaris.*
13. Victory in war, *victoria belli.*
14. Devotion to us, *studium nostri.*
15. Grief for his son, *luctus filii.*
16. A means of guarding against troubles, *cautio incommodorum.*

NOTE. — Nouns which denote *feeling* often take the accusative with in, erga, adversus, ad, instead of an objective genitive. Prepositions are also used when the relation is very remote. (See examples under § **50**, 3. *d*).

b. Wherever the relation expressed by a noun with a preposition (especially OF) can be viewed *as a quality of the modified noun*, the Latin prefers to use an adjective : just as in English we say, *the Boston massacre; the Jackson administration; the Socratic philosophy; the touch of the royal hand*, &c. (compare examples in Lesson 5). Thus —

1. The shout of the enemy, *clamor hostilis.*
2. Jealousy of the Senate, *invidia senatoria.*
3. Confidence in you, *fiducia tua* (more commonly *tui*).
4. The Cyrus of Xenophon, *Cyrus Xenophonteus.*

c. Where a word denoting a whole is used with another denoting a part (English OF, IN, AMONG), it is regularly put in the genitive. (But notice carefully the Remarks on page 116 of the Grammar.) The peculiarities of the construction are seen in the following idiomatic phrases : —

1. Enough money, *satis pecuniae.*
2. More learning than wisdom, *plus doctrinae quam prudentiae.*
3. One of a thousand, *unus de multis.*
4. Alone of all, *solus ex omnibus* (or *omnium*).
5. At that age, *id aetatis.*
6. Nowhere in the world, *nusquam gentium.*
7. Of the two consuls one was killed and the other wounded, *duo consules alter est interfectus alter vulneratus.*

Exercise 14.

1. On his way[1] to prison Phocion suffered some[2] gross[3] insults from the populace with-meekness[4] and dignity.[5]   2. Two wives of the German king, Ariovistus, perished; of their daughters, one was slain, another captured.   3. We have not yet discussed[6] the principal wages of virtue and the greatest of the prizes that are held out to it.   4. From his boyhood[7] the Roman soldier was schooled to[8] habitual[9] indiffer-

---

[1] *cum duceretur.*   [2] *quidam.*   [3] *gravis.*   [4] *submisse.*
[5] *cum* (with abl.).   [6] *disserere de.*   [7] *a puero.*
[8] Ablative.   [9] *perpetuus.*

ence to [his own] life.   5. During[1] the holidays in
summer[2] the young men exercise themselves with[3]
sports.   6. To what a degree of brutality will excess
of misery debase human nature!   7. Cneius Lentu-
lus, a military tribune, said to the wounded consul,
"Lucius Æmilius, whom the gods ought to favor as
the only [person] free-from[4] the blame of this day's
disaster, take this horse while you have any remains
of strength.[5]   Do-not[6] add to the horror of this day[7]
by the death of a consul.   Even without that, there is
abundant [cause for] tears and mourning."   8. I will
recount the delights and pleasures in this age of
eighty-three, which I now take, and on account of
which men generally account me happy.   9. Many
inventions greatly facilitate success in the chase.   The
most singular of these is a poison in which they dip
their arrows.   The slightest wound with these envenomed shafts is mortal.   10. Hannibal, after his defeat
at Zama, served his country in peace.   11. Many men
expose themselves to death for the sake of power;
but this king resigned his crown because his love for
his dominion, his affection for his subjects, and his regard for their interests were greater than his desire for
power.   12. The conspirators divided into three parties.
One was posted near the governor's house, a second
secured the approaches to the market-place, a third
hastened to the quarter of the tombs, and awaited
the signal for the fight.   13. Not only was Brutus's
life saved at the battle of Pharsalus, but, restored to
the state after the death of Pompey, along with many
of his friends, he had also great influence with[8] Cæsar.

---

[1] Ablative.   [2] Adjective.   [3] *in.*   [4] *insons.*

[5] *dum aliquid superest virium.*   [6] *ne* (perf. subj.).

[7] Lit. "make this day one-of-horror" (*funestus*).   [8] *apud.*

Lesson 16.

Cases. — 7. Use of Two Cases.

1. REVIEW § **51**, 1. with *d* ; 2. with *c* (Accusative and Dative) ; § **52**, 2. with *a*, *b*, *c*, *d* (two Accusatives). Learn § **50**, 4. *a*, *b*, *c* (Verbs of Reminding, Accusing, &c., with the Impersonals **miseret**, &c.).

2. A verb in English, besides its object, has often another modifying noun with a preposition. Such nouns are in Latin usually put in the case corresponding to the English preposition, though sometimes a preposition is expressed.

a. The Accusative and Dative (compare Lesson 10, *b*), in such phrases as —

1. He laid the burden on my shoulders, *humeris meis onus imposuit.*
2. I do not envy Crassus for his wealth (I do not grudge wealth to Crassus), *Crasso divitias non invideo.*
3. Cæsar required ten hostages of the Helvetians, *Caesar Helvetiis decem obsides imperavit.*

NOTE. — In these cases notice the Latin idiom, as it often differs from the English ; and observe carefully the construction of each verb as given in the Vocabulary.

b. Accusative and Genitive, in such phrases as —

1. You remind me of my duty, *me mones officii.*
2. He accuses me of theft, *arguit me furti.*
3. I repent of my folly, *meae me stultitiae paenitet.*
4. I am weary of life, *me vitae taedet* (weary with toil, *fessus labore*).

c. Two Accusatives : 1. One in Apposition (see Lesson 2) ; 2. With verbs of Asking and Teaching :

Panætius taught Scipio the Greek philosophy, *Panaetius Scipionem Graecam docuit philosophiam.*

Exercise 15.

1. The men-of-Minturnæ[1] repented of their ungrateful conduct towards[2] a man who had been the safety of Italy. 2. The younger Marius put an end to his own life.[3] 3. In the proscriptions of Sulla, to many a man who belonged to no party an estate or a house was his destruction. For although the property of the proscribed belonged to the state, yet the friends of Sulla purchased it at-a-nominal-price.[4] 4. Marius upbraided the nobles[5] [with] their effeminacy and idleness, and proudly compared his own words and exploits with their indolence and ignorance. His election was a great victory for the common-people, and a great humiliation to the aristocracy. 5. The great numbers of the enemy were a hindrance rather than a help to them. 6. Polybius taught the noblemen of Rome their own municipal law. 7. O Jupiter! give us those things that are-good-for[6] us! 8. Praise is to an old man an empty sound. I have outlived my friends and my rivals. Nothing is now of much account to me. 9. An exile and a menial muttered the last farewell to Pompey, the mighty victor of the East, the powerful lord of the Roman Senate. 10. The Senate distributed provinces and suitable honors among the partisans of Brutus. 11. The noblest of the Romans were ashamed of the victory by which they had avenged the disgrace of the Caudine Forks. 12. Old age is[7] most irksome[7] to the poor.[8] 13. Publius Autronius and Servius Cornelius Sulla had been elected consuls, but were convicted of bribery. Catiline also, who wished to

[1] *Minturnensis.*   [2] *erga.*   [3] *mortem sibi consciscere.*
[4] *minimo.*   [5] Dative.   [6] *convenire.*   [7] *piget.*   [8] Accusative.

become a candidate, had been impeached[1] for oppression in his province by Publius Clodius. 14. Caius Mucius was seized by the guards and brought before the king, who threatened him with cruel tortures. But he said, " See now how little your torments terrify[2] me." Then he plunged his right hand into the fire of an altar that burned near by, and held it in the flames, by which it was wholly consumed. From this act the name *Scævola* was given him, which signifies *He that uses the left hand.* 15. The second secession extorted from the patricians again a second[3] great charter[4] of liberty. The people had become tired of the decemvirs, and were dissatisfied[5] with their measures; for which reason they retired from [their] office, and the people elected ten tribunes. The decemvirs were then accused of treason, and some were condemned to death, others committed suicide. Two consuls were elected, and the Valerian and Horatian laws were passed. The plebeians were still, however, debarred from marriage with the patricians.

[1] *reus fieri.* [2] Subjunctive. [3] *alter.* [4] *pignus.* [5] *paenitet.*

Lesson 17.

Cases. — 8. Time and Place.

LEARN § **55**, 1. with *a;* 2. and *b;* 3 (reading Note), with *a, b, c, d, f,* 2. and 4; also Remark under § **56**, 1. *c.*

a. Many expressions have in Latin the construction of *time when*, where in English time is not the main idea : as,

1. In the fight at Cannæ, *pugna Cannensi* (or *apud Cannas*).
2. At the Roman games, *ludis Romanis.*
3. In all the wars of Gaul, *omnibus Gallicis bellis.*

b. In many expressions of time the accusative with **ad, in,** or **sub,** is used. Such are the following : —

1. **A thanksgiving was voted for the 1st of January,** *suppli-catio decreta est in Kalendas Januarias.*
2. **They assembled at the** [appointed] **day,** *convenerunt ad diem.*
3. **Till evening,** / **Towards (about) evening,** } *ad vesperum.*
4. **About the same time,** *sub idem tempus.*

c. Time either *during* or *within which* may be expressed by a noun in the singular, with an ordinal numeral : as,

1. **Within (just) four days,** *quinto die.*
2. **He has reigned going on six years,** *regnat jam sextum annum.* But also —
3. **He has already reigned for six years,** *regnavit jam sex annos.*

d. Distance of time before or after any thing is variously expressed : as,

1. **Three years after,** *post* (or **before,** *ante*) *tres annos, post tertium annum, tres post annos, tertium post annum, tribus post annis, tertio post anno.*
2. **Three years after his banishment,** *tribus annis (tertio anno) post exsilium (post quam ejectus est).*
3. **Within the last three years,** *his tribus proximis annis.*
4. **A few years hence,** *paucis annis.*
5. **Three years ago,** *abhinc annos tres (tribus annis)*; *ante hos tres annos.*
6. **It is three years since,** *triennium est cum (tres anni sunt cum).*

e. The *time of day* is only counted by hours, beginning at sunrise (**primā, secundā horā**) ; the time of night by watches, (**vigiliae**), of which there were four from sunset to sunrise.

f. The names of the Months are adjectives, and agree either with **mensis** or with the parts into which the month was divided in the complicated Roman system, for which see Grammar, § **84.**

g. The year is expressed by the names of the *consuls* in the Ablative Absolute. Modern dates may be expressed by the year after the birth of Christ (*post Christum natum*).

h. With names of places (except Towns, &c., see § **55**, 3), TO is expressed by **in** or **ad** with the accusative ; IN by **in** or **ab**, with the ablative ; FROM by **ab**, **de**, **ex**, with the ablative. But AT, meaning *near* (not *in*), is expressed with all names of place by **ad** or **apud**, with the accusative.

REMARK. — Notice that, when several names of place follow a verb of motion, all must be under the same construction. Thus —

Within a few days after this was done the matter was reported to Chrysogonus in Sulla's camp at Volaterræ, *quadriduo quo haec gesta sunt res ad Chrysogonum in castra L. Sullae Volaterras defertur.*

Notice also that *the meaning of the Latin verb* must be considered in relations of place : as,

1. **He arrived in Spain,** *pervenit in Hispaniam.*
2. **He arrived at Rome,** *pervenit Romam.*
3. **They assembled in the Senate-house,** *convenerunt in curiam.*
4. **He brought his army together in one place,** *coëgit exercitum in unum locum.*

Exercise 16.

1. After the death of Lucretia, Brutus threw off his assumed stupidity, and placed himself at the head[1] of her friends. They carried the body into the market-place [of]Collatia.[2] There[3] the people took up arms and renounced the Tarquins. A number-of[4] young men attended the funeral-procession[5] to Rome. Brutus summoned the people[6] [and] related[7] the deed-of-shame.[8] All classes were influenced with the same indignation.[9] By order of the people Tarquin was deposed,[10] and, along with his family, was banished from the city. Brutus now set out for the army at Ardea.[11] Tarquin in the meantime had hastened to

[1] Lit. "added himself as leader."   [2] Accusative.   [3] Relative.
[4] *plures.*   [5] *exsequiae funeris.*   [6] *convocato populo.*
[7] *narrare de.*   [8] *facinus flagitiosum.*   [9] *dolor et indignatio.*
[10] *regnum abrogari* (with dat.).   [11] Accusative.

Rome, but found the gates closed against him. Brutus was received with joy at Ardea, and the army renounced [their] allegiance [1] to the tyrant. Tarquin, with his two sons, Titus and Aruns, took refuge at Cære, in Etruria. Sextus fled to Gabii, where he was shortly after murdered by the friends of those whom he had put to death. Tarquin had reigned twenty-two years when he was driven from Rome. In memory of this event an annual festival was celebrated on the 24th of February, called the *Regifugium.*

2. Jugurtha was taken prisoner. The [2] great traitor fell by the treachery of his nearest relatives. Lucius Sulla brought the crafty and restless Numidian in chains, along with his children, to the Roman headquarters; and the war, which had lasted for seven years, was at an end. The glory of this victory was given to Marius. King Jugurtha, in [4] royal robes and in chains, along with his two sons, preceded the triumphal chariot of the victor, when-he-entered [5] Rome two years afterwards, on January 1st, B. C. 104. By order of Marius, the son [6] of the desert perished a few days afterwards in the subterranean city prison.

---

[1] *obedientiam abicio.*   [2] *ille.*   [3] *vinctus catenis.*
[4] *regie vestitus.*   [5] Participle.   [6] *alumnus.*

Lesson 18.

Cases. — 9. Prepositions.

1. Learn § **56**, 1. with *a, b, c*; 2. comparing § **42**, 1. *a, b, c*, and 3 (Use of Prepositions); also § **52**, 1. *d;* 2. *b* (compounds of **circum** and **trans**).

2. In general, the use of prepositions in Latin is the same as in English. They are always followed

either by the Accusative or Ablative: those implying
motion towards an object for the most part taking the
accusative, and those implying *rest in*, or *motion
from an object*, the ablative.

NOTE. — There are very many idiomatic uses of prepositions,
for which see the Examples in § **42**, 2. and consult the Lexicon.

a. Position is frequently expressed in Latin with **ab** (rarely
ex), properly meaning *from :* as,

1. **In the rear,** *a tergo.*
2. **On the side of Pompey,** *a parte Pompeiana.*
3. **On the left hand,** *a sinistra* (compare **hinc,** *on this side*).
4. **On the other side,** *ex altera parte.*
5. **In a great degree,** *magna ex parte.*

b. In the choice of prepositions the Latin point of view must
be carefully observed, as in many cases it differs from our own
(see Remark under § **56**, 1. *c*). Thus —

1. **To put clothes into a chest,** *ponere vestes in arca.*
2. **To choose in one's place,** *in alicujus locum deligere.*
3. **To fight on horseback,** *ex equo pugnare.*
4. **It was reported in camp,** *in castra nuntiatum est.*
5. **To go on board ship,** *conscendere in navem* (more commonly without the preposition).
6. **To send a man a letter,** *mittere (dare) literas ad
   aliquem.* But —
7. **To give one a letter** (to carry), *dare literas alicui.*

c. In many cases where a preposition is used in English, Latin
has the preposition compounded with a verb or implied in it. In
such cases the construction of the Latin verb must be observed
(see Vocabulary) : as,

1. **To go over a river,** *flumen transire.*
2. **To take one's forces across a river,** *copias flumen
   transducere.*
3. **To go beyond the boundaries,** *egredi fines* (or **out of**
   the city, *ex urbe*).
4. **To fly from the enemy,** *fugere hostes.*
5. **To get into one's favor,** *inire alicujus gratiam.*

NOTE. — When a verb with a Preposition in English is represented in Latin by one of the compounds of § **51**, 2. *d* (**ad, ante, con**, &c.), it is commonly followed by the dative. If, however, the compound represents a verb qualified by an Adverb, it retains its original construction : as, **insidet equo,** *he sits upon a horse;* but, **convocat suos,** *he calls his men together.*

Exercise 17.

1. Without intelligence and goodness bodily gifts are [1] of little [2] worth.[1]

2. Besides life and sense (which he has in common with [3] the brutes), there is in man [4] something more exalted, more pure, and that more nearly approaches [5] to divinity.

3. It was an arduous [undertaking] to conduct such [6] a body of men through hostile nations, across swamps and rivers which had never been passed by any one except roving barbarians. But they penetrated a good way into the mountains. Then, however, a chief appeared, with a numerous body, in a narrow-pass. But men who had surmounted so many obstacles despised the opposition of such feeble enemies.

4. As I was hurrying through the town a group of boys ran before me, crying out, *Agamemnon! Agamemnon!* I went on behind them, and they led me to the tomb of the king of kings, a gigantic structure,[7] for the most part in-good-preservation,[8] of a conical form, and covered with turf. The stone over the door is twenty-seven feet long [9] and seventeen wide ; larger than any hewn [10] stone in the world, except Pompey's pillar. The royal sepulchre was forsaken and empty ; the shepherd shelters his flock within it ; the traveller sits under its shade, and at-that-moment [11] a goat was

---

[1] *valere.* [2] Superlative. [3] *commune esse [alicui] cum.* [4] Plural.
[5] *prope abesse.* [6] *tantum agmen.* [7] *moles.* [8] *incolumis.*
[9] *in longitudinem.* [10] *quadratus.* [11] *tum maxime.*

dozing¹ quietly in [one] corner. I turned-away²
[and] left him³ in quiet possession. The boys were
waiting outside the door, and crying, *Mycenæ! Mycenæ!* led me away from the place.

5. I have at length arrived at Cadiz. I came
across the bay yesterday morning, and have established myself in very pleasant rooms which look out
upon the public square of the city. The morning sun
awakes me, and the sea-breeze comes in at my
window. At night the square is lighted by lamps
suspended from the trees, and thronged with a brilliant
crowd of the young and gay. Cadiz is beautiful
almost beyond-imagination.⁴

¹ *dormito* (imperfect).   ² Participle.   ³ Relative.
⁴ *supra quam quis animo concipere possit.*

Lesson 19.

Verbs. — 1. Narrative Tenses.

1. LEARN § **58**, 1. 2. with *a*, *d*; 3. with *a*, *c*;
5, 6 (Present and Past Tenses of the Indicative);
§ **57**, 8. *h* (Historical Infinitive). Also, review § **27**, 3
(use of the Perfect and Imperfect).

2. The narrative tenses in Latin are used nearly as
in English. But —

a. The Present is used much oftener than in English to express
a past action more vividly.

b. The ordinary English past tense is represented in Latin
sometimes by the Perfect (historical), and sometimes by the Imperfect. (For the distinction see § **27**, 3.) But the use of
the Imperfect depends not so much on the actual duration
of the action as upon the way in which the writer wishes to
represent it. Thus —

1. Cicero lived sixty-three years, *Cicero vixit LXIII annos.* [Here the action, though of long duration, is stated as a simple fact.]
2. Bibulus watched the heavens, while Cæsar held the election, *Bibulus de caelo servabat, cum Caesar comitia habebat,* or *habuit.* [Here the action, though brief, is represented as continuing.]
3. Homer flourished before the founding of Rome, *Homerus fuit ante Romam conditam.*
4. Homer was more skilled than Hesiod, *Homerus doctior erat Hesiodo.*

c. In rapid narrative, the English past tense is often rendered by the simple (historical) Infinitive, with its subject in the nominative. This construction also often corresponds with the English "began to." (For examples, see Grammar, p. 156.)

d. Customary action is represented in general by the Present, and in past tense by the Imperfect; though **soleo**, and similar words, are often used (but much less commonly than in English) to give emphasis to the fact of custom. Thus —

1. He was always praising Milo, *laudabat semper Milonem.*
2. He would often play with his children, *saepe cum pueris ludebat.*
3. It was a habit of Quintus Mucius to tell, *Q. Mucius narrare solebat.*

e. The beginning of an action is often expressed by the Present or Imperfect, especially with **jam**: as,

1. I begin to feel like dancing, *jam lubet saltare.*
2. They stood up and began to applaud, *stantes plaudebant.*

f. The English compound perfect is often expressed in Latin (when the action still continues) by the present, with some word denoting duration of time. The same usage with the imperfect is more rare.

1. We have suffered many years, *multos annos patimur.*
2. We have long been involved in dangers, *jam diu in periculis versamur.*
3. The forces which they had long been getting ready, *copiae quas diu comparabant.*

Exercise 18.

1. The Tiber had overflowed its banks far and wide.[1] The cradle in which the babes were placed was stranded at the foot of the Palatine, and overturned on the root of a wild fig-tree. A she-wolf, which had come to drink[2] of[3] the stream, came to them from time to time, and suckled them. When[4] they wanted other food, the woodpecker, a bird sacred to Mars, brought it to them. At length this marvellous spectacle was seen[5] by Faustulus the king's shepherd, who took the children home to his wife Acca Larentia. They were called Romulus and Remus, and grew up with the sons of their foster-parents[6] on the Palatine Hill.

2. Then Nasica rushed out of the Senate-house, followed[7] by many of the Senators. The people made[8] way for them, broke up[8] the benches, and armed[8] themselves with sticks, and rushed[8] upon Tiberius and his friends. The tribune[9] fled to the temple of Jupiter; but the door had been barred by the priests, and in his flight he fell over a prostrate body. As[10] he was rising, he received the first blow from one of his colleagues, and was quickly despatched.

3. Pyrrhus was at first victorious; for his own talents were superior to those of the captains who were opposed to him, and the Romans were not prepared for the onset of the elephants of the East, which were then for the first time seen in Italy — as it were moving mountains, with long snakes for hands. But the victories of the Epirots were fiercely disputed,

---

[1] *late.* [2] *potum* (supine). [3] *ad* (acc.). [4] *cum* (with indic.).
[5] *conspicere.* [6] *altores.* [7] *comitatus.* [8] Hist. Inf.
[9] *ille.* [10] *cum* (with imperf. subj.).

dearly purchased, and altogether unprofitable. At length Manius Curius Dentatus, who had in his first consulship won two triumphs, was again placed at the head of the Roman commonwealth, and sent to encounter the invaders. A great battle was fought near Beneventum, in which Pyrrhus was completely defeated.

4. Cato was an unfeeling and cruel master. His conduct towards his slaves was detestable. After dinner he would often severely chastise them, thong in hand, for some trifling act of negligence, and sometimes condemned them to death. When they were worn out or useless, he sold them or turned them out of doors. He treated the lower animals no better. His war-horse, which had borne him through his campaign in Spain, he sold in-that-country.[1] In his old age he sought gain with increasing eagerness, but never attempted to profit by the misuse of his public functions. He accepted no bribes, he reserved no booty to his own use; but he became a speculator, not only in slaves, but in buildings, artificial waters, and pleasure-grounds. In this, as in other points,[2] he was a representative of the old Romans, who were a money-getting[3] and money-loving[4] people.

[1] *ibi.*   [2] *res.*   [3] *quaestuosus.*   [4] *avarus.*

Lesson 20.

Verbs.— 2. The Passive Voice.

1. LEARN § **23**, 3 (use of the Passive); § **35**, 1. *b* (gerundive of Deponents); § **40**, *b* (second Periphrastic Conjugation).

Review § **51**, 4. *a*, *b* (dative of Agent); § **54**, 4 (ablative of Agent).

2. The Passive in Latin is often employed where in English we prefer the Active. The principal cases are the following : —

a. The Impersonal use of neuter verbs in the passive (compare § **39,** *c ;* and Method, Lesson 20, Obs. 3) : as,

1. They live on plunder, *ex rapto vivitur.*
2. They fought fiercely on both sides, *acriter utrimque pugnatum est.*

b. This impersonal use is the regular way of representing the English passive, where the corresponding Latin verb does not govern the accusative (see § **51,** 2. *f*) : as,

1. The commander is relieved (by the appointment of a successor), *imperatori succeditur.*
2. I am persuaded that this is true, *mihi persuasum est hoc esse verum.*
3. These things are done more easily than they are resisted, *facilius haec fiunt quam his resistitur.*
4. This subject was much discussed, *de hac re multum disputatum est.*
5. Let the influence of friends be employed, and when employed obeyed, *amicorum auctoritas adhibeatur et adhibitae pareatur.*

c. The most common way of expressing the English *ought, must,* and the like, is by some form of *esse* with the Gerundive, which in this construction is always PASSIVE, no matter which voice is used in English (compare § **73,** 2. Note) : as,

1. Nobody is to be blamed, *nemo culpandus est.*
2. We must do every thing, *omnia nobis sunt facienda.*
3. All must die, *omnibus moriendum est.*
4. We must resist old age (or old age must be resisted), *senectuti resistendum est.*

d. When the Subject of the action is indefinite, the Latin generally prefers the passive construction (compare *a,* above) : as,

1. Men do not gather grapes from thorns, *ex sentibus uvae non percipiuntur.*
2. We do ill whatever we do from confidence in fortune, *male geritur quicquid geritur fortunae fide.*

e. Many neuter verbs in English are rendered in Latin by reflexives or by the passive: as,

1. Hens roll in the dirt, *gallinae in pulvere volutantur.*
2. He rides on the Appian Way, *in via Appia vehitur.*
3. Codrus is bursting with envy, *invidia rumpitur Codrus.*
4. He turns to his lieutenant, *ad legatum se vertit* (or, *vertitur*).

3. On the other hand, an active construction is often preferred in Latin, where the passive is used in English. This happens —

a. In cases where the emphasis is on the Object of an action, or the action itself, rather than on the Agent ; because the emphasis can be given in Latin (though not in English) by position. Thus —

1. Socrates was put to death by his fellow-citizens, *Socratem cives sui interfecerunt.*
2. Egypt is watered by the Nile, and Mesopotamia made fertile by the Euphrates, *Aegyptum Nilus irrigat, Mesopotamiam fertilem efficit Euphrates.*

b. As most deponent verbs have no passive, the active construction must frequently be used for the English passive : as,

1. He is most admired who is not influenced by money, *quem pecunia non movet eum homines maxime admirantur.*
2. We should not mourn a death which is succeeded by immortality, *non lugenda est mors quam immortalitas consequatur.*

c. In a few cases, instead of the regular passive in Latin, a neuter verb of kindred meaning is employed : as,

1. To add, *addere ;* to be added, *accedere.*
2. To destroy, *perdere ;* to be destroyed, *perire.*
3. To sell, *vendere ;* to be sold, *venire* (*veneo*).
4. To flog, *verberare ;* to be flogged, *vapulare.*

4. When the present passive in English denotes *a completed action*, it is generally represented by the perfect in Latin ; but when it denotes *an action in*

progress, or *a general fact*, we must use the present. Thus —

1. The enemy are beaten, *hostes victi sunt.*
2. He is loved by his friends, *diligitur ab amicis.*
3. Among the Parthians the signal is given by a drum, *apud Parthos signum datur tympano.*

REMARK. — Care must be taken in rendering the confused or disguised forms of the passive in English : as,

1. The house is building, *domus aedificatur* (but, he is building a house, *domum aedificat*).
2. While these things are being done, *dum haec geruntur.*

5. When a verb in the active voice is followed by two cases (with or without a preposition), the accusative of the direct object becomes the subject of the passive, the other case being retained as in the active construction. Thus (compare examples on p. 37) —

1. Crassus is not envied for his wealth, *Crasso divitiae non invidentur.*
2. Verres is charged with extortion, *Verres repetundarum reus fit.*
3. Cato is asked his opinion, *Cato rogatur sententiam.*

REMARK. — The use of a second accusative in this construction is found chiefly with **rogo, posco,** and **celo.**

Exercise 19.

1. We must resist old age, my friends, — says Cicero in the book entitled [1] *Cato Major*, — and its failings must be made good by pains-taking. We must fight against old age as against disease. Regard must be paid to health. Moderate exercise should be employed, a sufficiency of food and drink must be taken.[2] Not only the body needs to be bolstered-up, but the mind and soul much more ; for these too die out through old age.

[1] See Lesson 8. 3.   [2] *adhibere.*

2. "Even now," said Cæsar, "we may[1] return ; if we cross the bridge, arms must decide the contest." At that moment of suspense[2] [there] appeared suddenly the figure of a youth, remarkable for comeliness and stature, playing on a pipe, the emblem of peace and security. The shepherds who were about the spot began to mingle with the soldiers and straggle towards him, captivated by his simple airs ; when with a violent movement he snatched a trumpet from one of the military band,[3] rushed with it to the bank of the river, and blowing a furious blast of martial music, leaped into the water, and disappeared on the opposite side. "Let us advance,"[4] exclaimed Cæsar, "where[5] the gods direct, and our enemies invite us. Be the die cast!"

3. A conspiracy[7] against the life of Cæsar had-been-formed[7] in-the-beginning-of-the-year.[8] Many of the conspirators had fought in the war against Cæsar; and had not only been pardoned[6] by him, but raised to offices of rank and honor. Among others was Marcus Junius Brutus, whom Cæsar had pardoned after the battle of Pharsalia, and had since treated almost as a son. He was now persuaded by Cassius to-join[9] the conspiracy, and imitate his ancestor Lucius Junius Brutus, the liberator[10] of Rome from the tyranny of the Tarquins. They now resolved[11] to assassinate[9] the Dictator in the Senate-house on the Ides of March. Rumors of the plot got abroad, and Cæsar was strongly urged not to attend the session of

---

[1] *posse,* impersonal.   [2] *in ea sollicitudine.*
[3] *uni ex cornicinibus.*   [4] Present Subjunctive.   [5] *qua.*
[6] Change the voice.   [7] Impersonal.   [8] *ineunte anno.*
[9] *ut,* with imper. subj.   [10] Lit. "who," &c.   [11] Impers. passive.

the Senate. But he disregarded the warnings which had been given him.

4. The ten ambassadors, of whom Cato was chief, offered their arbitration, which was accepted by Masinissa, but rejected by the Carthaginians, who had no confidence in Roman justice. This refusal Cato never forgave them. In traversing their country, he had remarked the increasing wealth and population. After his return to Rome, he let fall from the fold of his robe some early-ripe Libyan figs; and as[1] their[2] beauty was admired,[1] "Those figs," quoth he, "were gathered three days ago at Carthage. So close is our enemy to our walls." From that time forth, whenever he was called upon for his vote in the Senate, though[3] the subject of debate bore no relation to Carthage, he added these words, "Carthage must be destroyed."

[1] Active (*cum*, with imperf. subj.).   [2] Relative.
[3] *quamquam*, with imperf.

Lesson 21.

Verbs. — 3. Infinitive Constructions.

1. LEARN § **57**, 8. with *a*, *b*, *c* (uses of the Infinitive); also § **58**, 11. with *a*, *b* (use of the Present and Perfect infinitive); also §§ **57**, 8. *e;* **67**, 1 (Indirect Discourse).

2. The English infinitive is rendered by the Latin infinitive in many constructions: —

a. When it is equivalent to an abstract noun: as,

To err is human, *humanum est errare.*

NOTE. — An abstract noun is also sometimes equivalent to an infinitive, and is to be rendered in the same way in Latin: as,

1. What is creation? *Quid est creare?*
2. Writing with a stile is easy, *est facile stilo scribere.*

b. When a second action of the same subject is indicated : as, **I begin to grow old, *senescere incipio.***

NOTE. — This principle includes many classes of words where the connection is very close between the infinitive and the verb on which it depends ; and also many where it is more remote, so that a subjunctive clause might also be used.

3. The English THAT with a verb, when it denotes a statement or thought, is always to be rendered by *an Infinitive with an Accusative for its subject.* This construction (called the Indirect Discourse) is a very common one in Latin, and is used after all words of *knowing, perceiving, thinking, and telling.* In English we often use the infinitive in such sentences as the preceding : as, " I think it to be right ; " " He is said to be rich ; " and so on.

a. The English simple infinitive, with expressions of *hoping, promising, threatening,* and the like, is rendered by the same construction, of the infinitive with subject-accusative : as,

I hope to come, *spero me venturum* [*esse*].

b. The English infinitive may be used after any verb of *commanding or forbidding.* In Latin it is regularly used only after **jubeo** and **veto** (see hereafter, Lesson 28).

c. In using the Indirect Discourse in Latin, *observe what tense would be used in the direct discourse,* and make the tense of the infinitive correspond to that. Thus —

1. **He says that his father is here, *dicit patrem adesse.***
2. **He said that his father was here, *dixit patrem adesse.***
3. **He will say that his father is here, *dicet patrem adesse.***

In all these three cases the same tense is used in Latin, because the same tense would be used in the direct : viz. " My father is here."

4. **He says his father was here, *dicit patrem adfuisse.***
5. **He said his father had been (or was formerly) here, *dixit patrem adfuisse.***
6. **He will say that his father was here, *dicet patrem adfuisse.***

These three cases take the perfect infinitive, because the words in direct discourse would be, " My father was here."

7. **He says that his father will be here,** *dicit patrem adfuturum* [*esse*].

8. **He said that his father would be here,** *dixit patrem adfuturum.*

9. **He will say that his father will be here,** *dicet patrem adfuturum.*

In these cases, the words in direct discourse would be, " My father will be here." (In this tense, the **esse** is usually omitted.) In like manner, with verbs of *promising, expecting,* and the like —

10. **He hopes to come** (direct, "I shall come"), *sperat se venturum.*

11. **He hopes that you are well,** *sperat te valere.*

12. **He hopes that you were there,** *sperat te adfuisse.*

13. **He threatened to destroy the city,** *minatus est se urbem deleturum.*

d. When the verb of knowing, &c., is in the Passive, the impersonal construction is more common in English; but in Latin the personal is regular with the *simple* tenses, the impersonal with the *compound* (see § **70**, 2. *a*) : as,

1. **It seems to me that you are wrong,** *videris mihi errare.*

2. **It was reported that Cæsar's house had been attacked,** *oppugnata domus Caesaris nuntiabatur.*

3. **There is a tradition that Homer was blind,** *traditum est Homerum caecum fuisse.*

4. The subject of the Infinitive is regularly in the Accusative. But if the subject of the infinitive *is not expressed*, then any predicate word will agree with the subject of the main clause if there be a personal subject (see § **57**, 8. *e*, with Remarks) : as,

1. **It is advantageous to be honest,** *utile est probum esse.*

2. **I am anxious to be merciful,** *cupio me esse clementem* (or *cupio esse clemens*).

N. B. Never translate the infinitive of Purpose by the infinitive in Latin (see hereafter, Lesson 25).

The English Infinitive and the clause with THAT are also often to be rendered by other constructions than the above (for which see hereafter, Lesson 28).

Exercise 20.

1. "You," said Scipio Æmilianus, "to whom Italy is not mother, but step-mother, ought to keep silence. Surely you do not think that I shall fear those let loose whom I sent in chains to the slave-market."

2. The king of Syria, Antiochus, had nearly conquered Egypt. Popilius Læna ordered him, in the name of the Senate, to abandon the country. Antiochus wished to deliberate; but Popilius, having traced[1] a circle[1] about the king with a staff which he held in his hand, "Before[2] leaving this circle," said he, "answer the Senate." Antiochus promised to obey, and went out of Egypt. Popilius then divided the kingdom between the two brothers Philometor and Physcon.

3. I purpose[3] to write the history of a memorable revolution which has agitated men deeply, and which divides them even to-day. I do not conceal from myself the-difficulties-of-the-undertaking;[4] for passions which it was thought were stifled under [the influence of] a military despotism have just been reawakened. Suddenly men overwhelmed with years and toil have felt revive[5] in them resentments which seemed to be appeased, and have communicated them to us their children and heirs. But if we have-to-maintain[6] the same cause, we-have-not[7] to defend their conduct;

---

[1] Participle passive, ablative absolute (see next Lesson).
[2] *ante quam*, with future.   [3] *in animo habere.*
[4] Lit. " how difficult are (subj.) those things which I undertake."
[5] Infinitive.   [6] Part in *dus*, agreeing with *causa.*
[7] *nihil opus est.*

and we can separate liberty itself from those who have well or ill served it, while [1] we still have the advantage of-having-heard [2] and watched these old men, who, filled as-they-are [3] with their memories still excited by their impressions, teach us to understand them.

4. The king entered the ship in a violent storm, which the mariners beholding-with-astonishment,[4] at length with great humility gave him warning of the danger. But he commanded them instantly to put off, and not be afraid, for he had never in his life heard that any king was drowned.

[1] *cum*, with subj.　　[2] *quod*, with indic.　　[3] *quidem.*
[4] *admirari.*

Lesson 22.

Verbs. — 4. Participial Constructions.

1. LEARN § **72**, with 1. and *c;* 2, 3. with Remark and *a* (uses of Participles). Also, 4. with *a;* with § **40**, *a*, *b* (Periphrastic Conjugations) ; § **72**, 5. with *a*, *b*, *c;* and § **54**, 10. *b* (Ablative Absolute).

2. The English participle is often expressed not by a participle in Latin, but by a relative clause, or one with **cum** or **dum** (see § **72**, 1. *c*) : as,

1. In the following winter, *ea quae secuta est hieme.*
2. Cæsar, seeing this, gave the signal for battle, *Caesar cum hoc vidisset signum dedit proelii.*
3. While humoring the young, I have forgotten that I am old, *dum obsequor adulescentibus, me senem esse oblitus sum.*

3. On the other hand, almost any simple modifying clause can be rendered in Latin in a participial form. This principle includes, among others, relative clauses,

and those introduced by *when, if, because, although,* together with many adverbial phrases.

a. If there is any word in the main clause to which the participle can be attached as a modifier, it usually agrees with it. This corresponds to the English use of participles, except that it is much more common.

1. Any evil is easily crushed at its birth, *omne malum nascens facile opprimitur.*

2. The enemy slay Valerius while fighting bravely, *Valerium hostes acerrime pugnantem occidunt.*

b. If there is no word to which the participle can be attached, the participle is put in the ablative, with some word in agreement, which serves as a kind of Subject (Ablative Absolute : see examples in " Method," p. 51).

c. Even what in English seems a separate clause is in Latin often crowded into the main clause in a participial form : as,

1. Our men followed them close — encumbered as they were — and cut them down, *quos impeditos nostri consecuti occiderunt.*

2. It is a wretched thing to fret yourself when it does no good, *miserum est nihil proficientem angi.*

d. The perfect active participle, which is missing in Latin, is supplied either (1) by a change of voice with the Ablative Absolute ; or (2) by a clause with **cum** or **dum**. The difficulty is, however, often avoided by the use of Deponents, whose perfect participle usually has an active signification. Thus —

1. Having delayed a little, and set fire to all the villages, they pushed forward, *paulisper morati, omnibus vicis incensis, contenderunt.*

2. Having observed this, he sent the third line as a relief to our men who were in difficulty, *id cum animadvertisset, tertiam aciem laborantibus nostris subsidio misit.*

Exercise 21.

1. Veii was not succored by the other Etruscan cities then threatened with an invasion of the Gauls. Besides, the Veians had given themselves a king

instead of the annual magistrate, and a king odious to the other cities. This lucumo, irritated at[1] not having been named chief of the confederation, had stirred up the artisans, and violently interrupted the sacred games of Volsinii. On leaving for the siege of Veii, the Roman knights swore never to return, unless [they were] conquerors. This was also the vow of the Spartans on leaving for Ithome. On[2] the approach of the Roman army, the Veians left their city, clothed in funeral apparel, and bearing lighted torches. The city was taken by a mine. The besiegers, [who were] concealed in it[3] near the temple of Juno, overheard the reply of an oracle, which the Etruscans had consulted. "Victory," said the priest, "shall be with[4] him who shall sacrifice this heifer on the altar." Then the Roman soldiers burst into the temple, seized the axe from the priest's hand, and struck down the heifer; and the town, thus betrayed by its own gods, fell into the hands of the Romans.

2. The deputation arrived at Epidaurus the peculiar seat of Æsculapius, and invited the god to make his abode at Rome. Nor did he refuse; for one of the snakes sacred to Æsculapius crawled from his temple to the city of Epidaurus, and thence proceeded to the sea-shore, and climbed up into the ship of the Roman ambassadors [which was] drawn up on the beach. They now, instructed by the Epidaurians that the god willingly accompanied them, sailed away with the sacred snake to Italy. But when[5] the ship stopped[5] at Antium — so goes the story — the snake left[6] [it and] crawled to the temple of Æsculapius

---

[1] Accusative with Infinitive.   [2] Ablative.   [3] Relative.
[4] Dative.   [5] Lit. "the ship (acc.) stopping."   [6] Participle.

in that city ; where he coiled himself round a tall palm-tree, and remained for three days.   The Romans meanwhile anxiously awaited his return to the ship. At last he went [1] back [and] did not move again till the ship entered the Tiber.   Then, when she came [2] to Rome, he again crawled forth, swam to the island in the middle of the Tiber, and there went on shore and remained quiet.   A temple was built, therefore, to the god on the spot which he had himself chosen.

[1] Participle.   [2] Pluperf. subj. (impers.).

Lesson 23.

Verbs.—5. Gerundive Constructions.

1. LEARN § **73**, 1, 2, 3. with *a, b, c, d* (use of the Gerund and Gerundive).

2. The English participial noun, or verbal in -ING, is represented in Latin in several different ways.

a. When it is subject or object, by the Infinitive (see Lesson 21), or **quod** with the Indicative ; rarely by a verbal noun : as,

1. **Your being here is agreeable,** *quod ades* (or *te adesse*) *gratum est.*
2. **I prefer writing to speaking,** *malo scribere quam loqui.*

b. In the other cases, most commonly by the Gerund or Gerundive ; less commonly by an Adverbial or Substantive Clause (see Lessons 25, 27) : as,

1. **The labor of writing is irksome,** *labor scribendi molestum est.*
2. **A plan was formed for firing the city,** *consilium inflammandae urbis initum est.*
3. **I dissuaded him from going,** *ne iret dissuasi.*

NOTE. — The Gerund and Gerundive are precisely equivalent in meaning.   But the Gerundive, being in its origin a passive construction, can be used only of verbs which govern the accusative (except **utor,** &c.).   When it can be used, it is generally to be preferred.

c. The phrase " without doing any thing," or the like, has no corresponding expression in Latin ; but must be analyzed and rendered by some other form of words, chiefly a participle or the ablative absolute : as,

1. **Without accomplishing his purpose,** *re infecta.*
2. **Without being compelled,** *non coactus.*
3. **He went away without doing this,** *abiit neque hoc fecit.*
4. **You shall not go without doing this,** *non abibis nisi hoc feceris.*
5. **I trod on a snake without knowing it,** *anguem calcavi insciens* (or *inscienter*).

d. Purpose is often expressed in Latin by the accusative of the Gerund or Gerundive with **ad**, or by the Genitive followed by **causā** or **gratiā** (see hereafter, Lesson 26, and examples, Grammar, page 183).

Exercise 22.

1. When polished nations have obtained the glory of victory, or have enriched themselves by the addition-of[1] territory, they may[2] end the war with honor. But savages are not satisfied until they extirpate[3] the community which is the object of their rage. They fight not to[4] conquer, but to[4] destroy. If they engage in hostilities, it is with a resolution never to-see[5] the face of the enemy in peace, but to prosecute the war with immortal enmity. The desire of vengeance [is] the first and almost the only [principle which] a savage instils into the minds of [his] children.

2. Cato's opinion prevailed, and the Senate only waited for a favorable opportunity to-destroy[5] the city. The Romans had resolved on war ;[6] and when the Carthaginian ambassadors arrived at Rome, to[4] offer to the Senate the submission of Carthage, the two consuls were already levying troops. The ambassa-

---

[1] Gerundive.   [2] *licet.*   [3] Perfect.   [4] *ad*, with gerund.
[5] Gen. of gerund.   [6] *bello decertare statuerant.*

dors, knowing that resistance was hopeless, sought[1] to appease the anger of the Senate by unconditional obedience. They were ordered to send three hundred of the noblest families to [meet] the consuls at Lilybæum, and were told that the consuls would inform them of the further orders of the Senate.

3. Sulla, [when] quaestor in the war against-Jugurtha,[2] by his zeal and energy soon gained the full approval of [his] commander. He was equally successful in gaining the affections of the soldiers. He always addressed them with the greatest kindness, seized every opportunity of conferring favors upon them, was ever ready to[3] take-part-in all the jests of the camp, and at the same time never shrank from sharing in all their labors and dangers. It is a curious circumstance that Marius gave to his future enemy and the destroyer of his family and party the first opportunity of distinguishing himself. The enemies of Marius claimed for Sulla the glory of the betrayal-of[4] Jugurtha; and Sulla himself took the credit of it by always wearing a signet ring representing[5] the scene of the surrender.

---

[1] *conor.* [2] Adjective. [3] *ad*, with gerundive.
[4] Perf. part. [5] Lit. "on which was represented."

Lesson 24.

Verbs. — 6. Subjunctive Constructions.

1. LEARN § **57**, 2. with *a, b;* 3, 4, 5, 6 (uses of the Subjunctive); also 7. with *a* (Imperative Constructions).

2. The Subjunctive mood in Latin is used to represent a great variety of constructions in English, most

of which are included in the dependent clauses, to be given in future Lessons. The others are the following : —

a. The rare Subjunctive in English is for the most part rendered by the subjunctive in Latin (but compare special constructions in future Lessons). Thus —

1. **Let him that standeth take heed lest he fall,** *caveat qui stat ne cadat.*
2. **I care not, so it serve the state,** *nil mea refert dummodo rei publicae prosit.*
3. **What would Cicero say if he were alive?** *Quid diceret Cicero si viveret?*

b. The auxiliaries which form the English Potential — *may, might, could, would, should* — are very loose in their use and meaning, being sometimes pure auxiliaries, and sometimes retaining their proper force. In the former case they are generally rendered by the subjunctive in Latin ; in the latter, they require some verb of similar meaning. Thus —

1. **You may say (it is possible you should say),** *dicas.*
2. **You may say (you are permitted to say),** *licet dicere.*
3. **He would go if I should wish it,** *eat si velim.*
4. **He would go (now) if I wished it,** *iret si vellem.*
5. **You would have it so,** *sic voluisti.*
6. **I should like to go,** *ire velim.*
7. **I could wish he were here,** *vellem adesset.*
8. **A soldier should obey his commander,** *miles imperatori parere debet.*
9. **Whoever could go went,** *quicumque ire poterat ivit.*
10. **What could I do (what was I to do)?** *Quid facerem?*
11. **I wish he would come,** *utinam veniat.*
12. **Would he were now here!** *O si nunc adesset!*

c. The English Imperative — except *commands in the second person* — is regularly rendered by the Latin subjunctive. Commands addressed to a definite person take the imperative in Latin ; prohibitions to a definite person, 1. **noli**, with the infinitive ; 2. **cave**, with the present subjunctive ; 3. **ne**, with the perfect subjunctive. Thus —

1. Let us go, *eamus.*
2. Well, be it so, *fiat sane.*
3. Let justice be done though the heavens fall, *fiat justitia ruat caelum.*
4. Leap down, fellow-soldiers, *desilite, commilitones.*
5. Do not suppose, *nolite putare.*
6. Pardon nothing, do nothing by favor, be not moved by compassion, *nihil ignoveris, nihil gratiae causa feceris, misericordia commotus ne sis.*

   d. General precepts, both affirmative and negative, are regularly expressed by the second person of the present subjunctive, less commonly the perfect.

   e. There are many idiomatic constructions — more especially clauses of Result and clauses in Indirect Discourse — which in Latin require the subjunctive, though they have no modal form in English. (For these constructions, see hereafter, especially Lessons 26 and 28.)

Exercise 23.

1. " Let him go then," they said, " where he pleases as an exile, and suffer in some other place whatever fate has reserved for him; and let us pray that the gods visit us not with their anger, for rejecting Marius from our city in poverty and rags." Moved by such considerations, all in a body entered the room where Marius was, and getting round him, began to conduct him to the sea.

2. " Why," said Rasselas, " should you envy others so great an advantage? All skill ought to be exerted for universal good. Every man has owed much to others, and ought to repay the kindness that he has received."

3. Sweet language will multiply friends, and a fair-speaking tongue will increase kind greetings. Be in peace with many; nevertheless have but one counsellor of a thousand. If thou wouldest [1] get a friend, prove

---

[1] *volo.*

him first, and[1] be not[1] hasty[2] to credit him. For some[3] man is a friend for[4] his own occasion,[4] and[5] will not[5] abide in the day of thy trouble.

4. My lords,[6] if you must fall may you so fall. But if you stand — and stand I trust you will — together with the fortunes of this ancient monarchy, — together with the ancient laws and liberties of this great and illustrious kingdom, — may you stand as unimpeached in honor as in power. May you stand the refuge of afflicted nations! May you stand a sacred temple for the perpetual residence of an inviolable justice!

5. Believe me, Athenians! if, recovering from this lethargy, you would[7] assume the ancient spirit and freedom of your fathers, the world might[7] once more behold you playing a part worthy of Athenians! May the gods inspire you to determine upon such measures!

6. Lay hold on this chance of safety, Conscript Fathers! by the immortal gods I conjure you. Give one sign to the Roman people, that even as now they pledge their valor, so you pledge your wisdom to the crisis of the state. Do you not know this Antony? Do you not know his companions? To be slaves to such as he, to such as they, would it not be the fullest measure of misery, joined with the fullest measure of disgrace? If it be so — which heaven forfend! — that[8] the supreme hour of the republic has come, let us, the rulers of the world, rather fall with honor than serve with infamy! Born to glory and to liberty, let us hold these bright distinctions fast, or let us greatly die!

---

[1] *neve.*   [2] Adverb.   [3] *quispiam.*   [4] *temporis causa.*
[5] *nec.*   [6] *Patres Conscripti.*   [7] Pres. subj.   [8] *ut*, with subj.

Lesson 25.

Relations of Time.

1. LEARN § **62**, with 2. *a*, *b*, and Remark 2 ; *c*, *d*, *e* (use of Temporal Particles) ; § **58**, 9, 10. with Remarks (Sequence of Tenses).

REMARK. — Whenever it becomes necessary to use the Subjunctive mood in a subordinate clause — as in this and the following Lessons — careful attention must be paid to the rule for the Sequence of Tenses. The learner must notice carefully *which is the main clause*, i. e., *what is the main fact to be stated.* This is often disguised in English by one or more modifying clauses ; especially Relative (WHO, WHICH), Temporal (WHEN), and Conditional (IF). Upon the time of the main clause will depend the time of the whole. Sometimes, however, an intervening dependent verb may throw the time back so as to require secondary tenses in those which follow, though the leading verb is primary. Thus —

1. **Cicero is said to have gone into exile to prevent civil war,** *Cicero ex patria excessisse dicitur ut bellum civile averteret.*

2. **We seem to have advanced so far that even in fulness of words we are not surpassed by the Greeks,** *tantum profecisse videmur ut a Graecis ne verborum quidem copia vinceremur.*

2. The English particle WHEN and similar expressions of time are rendered in Latin by two different constructions : — *a.* **ubi**, **postquam**, and similar particles (see 2. *a*) with the Indicative, usually the perfect ; *b.* **cum**, generally with the Indicative of the present or perfect, and with the Subjunctive of the imperfect or pluperfect (2. *b* : see examples in Grammar).

REMARK. — The distinction between these two constructions is not at first obvious ; but will become clearer by considering the distinction of Absolute and Relative time (see Note on page 177 of the Grammar), and by careful observation of the practice of Latin writers.

a. If WHEN is equivalent to WHENEVER, the Indicative is always to be used : as,

When midsummer had begun, he used to make his quarters at Syracuse, *cum aestas summa esse jam coeperat, Syracusis stativa faciebat.*

b. The common English form of narrative, " Such and such things had happened (were happening), WHEN," &c., is always to be rendered with the Indicative in Latin — usually with cum: as,

1. This he had said when news was brought, *dixerat hoc cum nuntiatum est.*

2. I was just reading your letters, when one was brought me, *legebam tuas epistolas, cum mihi epistola adfertur.*

c. If WHEN or WHILE approaches in meaning to SINCE (as it often does in fact), it is expressed by cum with the subjunctive ; sometimes by other constructions (see Lesson 22) : as,

But if you do not yet quite see — when the thing itself is plain by so many clear proofs and tokens, *quod si nondum satis cernitis — cum res ipsa tot tam claris argumentis signisque luceat.*

Exercise 24.

1. Hamilcar had poured the libation on the victim, which was duly offered on the altar ; when on-a-sudden he desired[1] all the others to[3] step aside to a little distance, [and then] called his son Hannibal. Hannibal, a boy of nine years old, went up to his father, and Hamilcar asked him kindly whether[2] he would like[2] to go with him to the war. When the boy eagerly caught at the offer and with a child's earnestness implored his father to[3] take him, Hamilcar took

---

[1] Participle.   [2] *velletne.*   [3] *ut,* with subj.

him by the hand and led him up to the altar; and
bade him, if he wished [1] to follow his father, to lay
his hand on the altar, and swear that he would never
be the friend of the Romans. Hannibal swore, and
never to his latest hour forgot his vow.

2. When [2] Archias came to the door of the temple
with his satellites, he found Demosthenes seated. He
first addressed him in language of friendly persuasion,
and offered to intercede with Antipater in his behalf.
Demosthenes, having listened for-a-time in silence to
his bland professions, at length replied, " Archias, you
never won me by your acting, nor will you now by
your promises." When the player found that he was
detected, he threw away the mask and threatened
in earnest. " Now," [3] said Demosthenes, " you speak
from the Macedonian tripod : before you were only
acting. Wait a little till I have written [4] a letter to my
friends at home." And he took a roll as if to write;
and, as was his wont when he was engaged in composition, put the end of the reed to his mouth, and bit
it; he then covered his head with his robe and bowed
his head.

3. When he had remained some time in this attitude, the barbarians, thinking that he was lingering
through fear, began to taunt him with cowardice; and
Archias, going up, urged [5] him to rise, and repeated
his offers of mediation. Demosthenes now [6] felt the
poison in his veins : he uncovered his face, and fixing
his eyes on the dissembler said, " It is time for you,
Archias, to finish the part of Creon, and cast my body
to the dogs. I quit thy sanctuary, Poseidon, still

[1] *si vellet.*   [2] *ubi.*   [3] *nunc.*   [4] Future perfect.
[5] *petere ab eo ut.*   [6] *jam.*

breathing; though [1] Antipater and the Macedonians have not spared even this from pollution." So saying, he moved with-faltering-step towards the door; but had scarcely passed the altar, when hc fell with a groan, and breathed his last.

[1] *cum*, with subj.

Lesson 26.

Purpose and Result.

1. READ carefully § **69**, comparing the references.

REMARK. — *a.* In general, Relative or other subordinate clauses aie used in Latin nearly as in English. But in Latin the Subjunctive mood is used in many such clauses, where English uses the Indicative. It will be seen, therefore, that not every relative or other subordinate clause is to be translated by the Latin subjunctive; nor, on the other hand, is every English indicative in such clauses to be rendered by the indicative. The learner must, accordingly, accustom himself to notice the true (logical) relation between the subordinate and the main clause ; and express the former according to the Latin idiom, which will appear in the subsequent Lessons.

b. When a relative clause (including those introduced by relative adverbs and conjunctions) simply states a fact or circumstance *which might be put as an independent statement*, there is no occasion for the subjunctive in Latin. But in most cases, where there is a logical relation between the two clauses, so that *the force of the relative clause would be lost* by taking it out of its connection with the former, the subjunctive is required in Latin.

N. B. Clauses expressing CAUSE — introduced in English by *because, since, inasmuch as* — take the subjunctive only in special idiomatic uses (see § **63**).

c. The most common uses of the subjunctive in clauses of the kind above referred to are to express PURPOSE — *in order that, that, to, in order to,* and the like ; or RESULT — *so that, that, so as to.*

2. LEARN § **64,** 1. with *a*, 2 (clauses of Purpose) ; § **65,** 1. with *a, b* (clauses of Result) ; 2. with *a, e, f* (clauses of Characteristic).

3. In English, relations of purpose and result are often expressed by the Infinitive, *which must never be used in this way in Latin.*

a. The most general way of expressing Purpose is by **ut** (negatively **ne**), unless the purpose is *closely connected with some one word,* in which case the relative is more common. Thus —

1. Arria gave her husband a sword in order that he might kill himself, *Arria gladium dedit marito ut se interficeret.*

2. Arria gave her husband a sword to kill himself with, *Arria gladium dedit marito quo se interficeret.*

b. The Gerundive constructions of Purpose are usually limited to short concise expressions, where the literal translation of the phrase, though not the English idiom, is nevertheless not harsh or strange.

c. The Supine in this construction is used only with verbs of motion and a few idiomatic expressions (see § **74,** 1). The Future Participle of Purpose should be avoided.

d. A kind of purpose is expressed idiomatically by the Gerundive used passively after particular verbs (see § **72,** 5. *c*).

e. In the greater number of cases Result is expressed by **ut** (negatively **ut non**), the relative being less common (compare examples in § **65,** 1).

f. The use of the Subjunctive in clauses of Characteristic (see § **65,** 2) can only be learned by practice and comparison of examples. But compare what is said above of Relative clauses in general.

g. Expressions such as " He is too honest to deceive," " It is too distant to be seen," and the like, which are very common in

English, are in Latin to be rendered by a clause of Result with
quam ut following a Comparative: as,

Cæsar was too merciful to punish his adversaries, *clemen-
tior erat Caesar quam ut inimicos puniret.*

Exercise 25.

1. On the reedy margin of the lake stood here and
there some monuments; tombs, it was said,[1] of ancient
Assyrian kings. As the royal galley, which Alexander steered himself, passed near one of them,[2] a
sudden gust of wind carried away his cap into the
water, and lodged the light diadem which circled it
on one of the reeds which grew out of the tomb. One
of the soldiers immediately swam out to recover it;[2]
and, to keep it dry, placed it on his own head. Alexander rewarded him with a talent; but at the same time
ordered him to be flogged for the thoughtlessness with
which he had assumed[3] the ensign of royalty. The
diviners, it is said, took the matter more seriously, and
advised the king to[4] inflict death on the offender,[5] in
order to avert the omen.

2. Socrates recommends to Alcibiades, in order
that he might have a model for his devotions, a short
prayer which a Greek poet composed for the use of
his friend in-the-following-words:[6] " O Jupiter! give
us those things which are good for us, whether they
are such things as we pray for or such things as we
do not pray for; and remove from us those things
which are hurtful, though they are such things as we
pray for."

3. Polybius also learned the Roman tongue, and
attained to that knowledge of their laws, their rights,
their customs and antiquities, that few of their own

[1] *dicebant.*   [2] Relative.   [3] Subjunctive.
[4] *ut,* with subj.   [5] *homo.* [6] *ita.*

citizens understood them better. So that he taught the noblemen of Rome their own municipal laws; and was accounted more skilful in them than Fabius Pictor, a man of the senatorial order, who wrote the transactions of the Punic wars. He who neglected none of the laws of history was so careful of truth that he made it his whole business to deliver nothing to posterity which might deceive them; and by that diligence and exactness [1] may be known to be studious of truth and a lover of it.

4. The Pompeians were too much dispirited to make any resistance. Shivered once more at the first onset, they poured in broken masses over hill and plain. But Cæsar was not yet satisfied. Allowing a part of his troops only to return to the camp, he led four legions in hot pursuit by a shorter and better road, and drew them up at a distance of six miles from the field of battle.

[1] *qua diligentia ac cura.*

Lesson 27.

Conditional Sentences.

READ carefully §§ **59, 60, 61,** including all the subsections, and committing to memory the types of conditional expressions on page 167.

a. The learner should notice carefully the precise nature of the condition which he wishes to render into Latin, because the use of the tenses in English is not uniform. Thus, — "If he is alive now" is a present condition, to be expressed in Latin by the Present Indicative; "If he is alive next year" is a future condition, and would be expressed by the Future Indicative. "If he were here now" is a present condition contrary to fact, and would be expressed by the Imperfect Subjunctive; "If he were to see me thus" is a future condition, to be expressed by the Present Subjunctive.

b. In cases where the Condition is omitted, it must be mentally supplied in order to determine the form of the condition.

c. The conditional phrases of Comparison, *as if, as though,* require in Latin the present and perfect subjunctive, not the imperfect and pluperfect, as in English (see Remark under § 61, 1).

d. For the Concessive expressions, *although, granting that, even if,* which require idiomatic constructions in Latin, see § 61, 2. For Provisos — *provided that, only let,* &c. — see § 61, 3.

Exercise 26.

1. Among the savages, to display undaunted fortitude in torments is the noblest triumph of a warrior. To avoid the trial by a voluntary death is deemed infamous and cowardly. If any one betrays symptoms of timidity, they often despatch him at once with contempt, as unworthy of-being-treated [1] like a man.

2. If we see a friend in distress, and give him all the consolation we are able, we perform the duties of friendship, which pays more attention to the disposition of the heart than to the value of the gift. A small present may be the testimony of a great love. There is no good I do not wish you, and this is all I can offer toward it. I wish this little treatise may be of use to you. If it should not answer my hopes, I shall, however, be secure of pardon from your friendship.

3. I am come to inform [2] you of a secret you must impart to Pausanias alone. From remote antiquity, I am of Grecian lineage. I am solicitous for the safety of Greece. Long since, but for the auguries, would Mardonius have given battle. Regarding these no longer, he will attack you early in the morning. Be prepared. If he change his purpose, remain as you are. He has provisions only for a few days more.

[1] See § 65, 2. *f.*   [2] See § 58, 10. *a.*

Should the event of the war prove favorable, you will but deem it fitting to make some effort for the independence of one who exposes himself to so great peril for the purpose of apprising you of the intentions of the foe. I am Alexander of Macedon.

4. After a short interval, Charles, turning to Philip, who stood awaiting his commands, thus addressed him : " If the vast possessions which are now bestowed on you had come by inheritance, there would be abundant cause for gratitude. How much more, when they come as a free gift in the life-time of your father ! But however large the debt, I shall consider it all repaid if you only discharge your duty to your subjects. So rule over them that men shall commend and not censure me for the part I am now acting."

5. We are here as in a theatre, where every one has a part allotted to him. The great duty which lies upon a man is to act his part in perfection. We may [1] indeed say that our part does not suit us, and that we could act another better. But this is not our business. All that we are concerned in is to excel in the part which is given us. If it be an improper one, the fault is not in us, but in Him who has cast our several parts, and is the great disposer of the drama.

[1] *possumus.*

Lesson 28.

Substantive Clauses.

1. READ carefully § 70, with Remark; 1, 2, 3, with *a, b, c, d, e, f* (substantive clauses of Purpose) ; 4. with *a, b, c, d, g, h* (clauses of Result); 5. with

b (clauses with **quod**). Compare § **57**, 8. *b*, *c*, *d*, and notice the general schedule of substantive clauses on page 249.

2. In English, one action depending upon another is in almost any case expressed indiscriminately by THAT or by the Infinitive. In Latin the form of expression will depend on *the meaning of the dependent words or clause.* This meaning can usually be determined by the following Rules : —

a. If the words can be put in an independent form *as the words of some person in the Indicative*, it is Indirect Discourse, and requires the Accusative with the Infinitive (see examples in § **70**, 2).

b. If they can be put in an independent form *as a Question*, they require the Subjunctive as Indirect Questions (see examples in § **67**, 2).

c. If they can be put in an independent form *as the words of some person in the Imperative*, or can be conceived as a Result, they require the Subjunctive. The Infinitive is used in many expressions of this class, either optionally or exclusively (see examples in § **70**, 3, 4).

d. If they could be expressed independently in the Indicative, but *as a fact*, and not as the words of some other person, they regularly require **quod** with the Indicative (see examples in § **70**, 5).

e. An English noun must often be rendered by a substantive clause, on account of the scarcity of abstract terms in Latin, or the want of a corresponding idiom. Thus —

1. **He was accused of treason against his country,** *accusatus est quod patriam prodidisset.*

2. **A value beyond all estimation,** *pretium majus quam ut aestimetur.*

f. In English a real substantive clause is often introduced by the common expression FOR with the Infinitive ; and is usually rendered in Latin by the Accusative and Infinitive : **ut** with the subjunctive is more rare. The meaning of the particular expression must be carefully noticed. Thus —

1. For a dying father to bequeath an empire to his son is a deed worthy of gratitude, *patrem morientem filio imperium legare factum est gratia dignum.*

2. The next thing is for me to speak of the war against the pirates, *reliquum est ut de bello dicam piratico.*

NOTE. — The forms of Indirect Discourse were developed in Latin into a very complex system, which, for the sake of fuller practice, will be exhibited in the two succeeding Lessons.

Exercise 27.

1. But before Cæsar allowed his tired soldiers to enjoy the fruits of the victory of Pharsalia he required them to complete the conquest. The pursuit was continued during the remainder of the day and on the morrow. But the task was easy.[1] The clemency of the conqueror induced all to submit. When Cæsar entered the camp, and saw the dead bodies of many Romans lying about, he exclaimed, " They would have it so. To have laid down our arms would have sealed our doom."

2. The soldiers of Viriathus recognized their general simply by his tall figure, and by his striking sallies of wit, and above all by the fact that he surpassed every one of his men in temperance as well as in toil.

3. The sailors were willing to do as he wished. But they were afraid that the vessel could not stand the beating of the waves, and as Marius also was much troubled with sickness, they made for land. They wandered about without any definite object, seeking merely to escape from the present evil as worst of all, and putting their hopes on the chances of fortune. For the land was their enemy, and the sea also; and they feared [2] to fall in with men, and

---

[1] Lit. " not difficult."

[2] Notice construction of verbs of fearing (§ **70**, 3. *f; * **57**, 8. *c*).

feared also not to fall in with men, because they were in want of provisions. After some time they met with a few herdsmen, who had nothing to give them in their need. But they recognized Marius, and advised him to get out of the way as quick as he could.[1]

4. Griselda, it is now time for you to reap the fruit of your long patience; and that they who have reported me to be cruel, unjust, and a monster in nature,[2] should know that what I have done has been all along with a view to teach you how to behave as a wife, and lastly to secure my own ease and quiet as long as we live [3] together, which I feared might have been endangered by my marriage. Therefore I had a mind [4] to prove you by harsh and injurious treatment; and not being aware that you have ever transgressed my will, either in word or deed, I now seem to have met with that happiness I desired. I intend then to restore in an hour what I have taken away from you in many; and to make you the sweetest recompense for the many bitter pangs I have caused you to suffer.

[1] Subjunctive.   [2] *ingenio.*   [3] Subjunctive.
[4] *mihi propositum habui.*

Lesson 29.
Intermediate Clauses.

LEARN § 66, with 1. *a, b, c, d,* and 2 (Intermediate clauses). Compare § 67, 1. and *b* (Subordinate clauses in Indirect Discourse).

REMARK. — Besides the constructions of dependent clauses already mentioned (which for the most part are suggested by some particle or some construction in English), another is found in Latin, which has no English equivalent whatever : namely, that of a clause subordinate to another *which is itself subordinate.* This is especially to be observed when any one of the Infinitive and Subjunctive expressions which have been treated under the head of substantive clauses — itself the subject or object of some leading verb — has another clause depending on it. In this case, the verb of the latter is almost invariably in the subjunctive. But, in applying the rule, the following conditions must be observed : —

a. When a subordinate clause depends on an infinitive or subjunctive, *so that it becomes logically a part of the same expression*, its verb must regularly be in the Subjunctive (see examples in § **66**, 2).

N. B. This rule does not apply to the case of a simple relative clause following a *complementary infinitive*, which will generally come under the following head.

b. If the subordinate clause is inserted for mere definition or explanation — so that it may be regarded as *true independently of the connection in which it stands* — its verb will be in the Indicative (see examples under § **67**, 1. *b*).

c. When a clause, though not depending on an infinitive or subjunctive, is represented as containing the words or thought *of any other person than the writer or speaker*, so that it becomes informal indirect discourse, the verb must be in the Subjunctive (see examples under § **66**, 1).

NOTE. — This construction is especially common in clauses expressing a reason or motive, which otherwise do not take the subjunctive.

d. A subordinate clause in a Conditional sentence will have the mood and tense of the principal verb.

Exercise 28.

1. Sulla, encouraging his soldiers, who were 35,000 men well armed, led them to Rome. The soldiers fell on the tribunes whom Marius had sent and murdered them. Marius also put to death many friends of Sulla in Rome, and proclaimed freedom to the slaves if they would join[1] him. But it is said that only three slaves accepted the offer.

[1] See *c*, above.

2. The next day Marius, compelled by hunger, and wishing to make use of his remaining strength before he was [1] completely exhausted, went along the shore, encouraging his followers, and entreating them not to abandon the last hope, for which he reserved [2] himself on the faith of an old prediction. For when he was quite a youth, and living in the country, he caught in his garment an eagle's nest as it was falling down,[3] with seven young ones [in it] ; which his parents wondering at, consulted the soothsayers, who told them that their son would become the most illustrious of men, and that it was [the will of] fate that he should receive the supreme command and magistracy seven times.

3. His attendants advised him to wait until he had made preparations of men and money. To which he only returned, "They that love me will follow me." In a few days he drove the enemy from before the city, and took the count prisoner ; who, raging at his defeat and calamity, exclaimed, "that this blow was from fortune ; but valor could make reprisals, as he should show, if he ever regained his liberty."

4. When with infinite toil they had climbed up the greater part of that steep ascent, Balboa commanded his men to halt, [and] advanced alone to the summit, that he might be the first who should enjoy a spectacle which he had so long desired.[4] As soon as he beheld the South Sea stretching in endless prospect below him, he fell on his knees, and, lifting up his hands to heaven, returned thanks to God, who had conducted [5] him to a discovery so beneficial to his country and so honorable to himself.

---

[1] See *a*, above.   [2] See *b*, above.   [3] *ad terram.*
[4] See *c*, above.   [5] See *b*, above.

Lesson 30.

Indirect Discourse.

READ attentively § **67**, throughout (Indirect Discourse), noticing carefully the Remark on page 187.

REMARK. — **1.** The Indirect Discourse in Latin corresponds to the common reporting of speeches, &c., in the newspapers and elsewhere, in which the *pronouns* and the *tenses of the verb* are changed, and the whole quotation is usually introduced by THAT, following a verb of saying, &c. This form of discourse is much more common and highly developed in Latin than in English, and may often be used in rendering the English direct narrative or quotation. Many difficulties and obscurities are avoided in Latin by the use of the reflexive pronoun, to refer to the speaker, and of the Indicative and Subjunctive moods as given in § **67**, 1. The rule defining the employment of these moods is as follows : —

a. The main clauses (statements) have their verbs in the Infinitive with the subject in the Accusative, as SUBSTANTIVE CLAUSES dependent on the verb of *saying*, &c. (see § **70**, 2).

b. Dependent clauses, introduced by relatives, relative or conditional particles, and the like, have their verbs in the Subjunctive, as INTERMEDIATE CLAUSES (see § **66**, 1).

c. Imperative forms of speech take the Subjunctive.

N. B. For special indirect forms see § **67**, 1. *c, d.*

d. The Subject of the verb must regularly be expressed in indirect discourse, though a pronoun omitted in the direct. References to the speaker must be made by the reflexives **se** and **suus.**

e. Repetitions of some verb of *saying*, &c., which are common in English for the sake of keeping up the form of indirect discourse, should be omitted in Latin.

f. Particular attention should be given in translating the *apodosis contrary to fact*, which is done by the future participle with **fuisse** (see examples in § **67**, 1. *c*).

g. Sequence of Tenses is very often violated in indirect discourse for the sake of greater vividness, by the use of primary instead of secondary tenses, — but never in a narrative clause with **cum**.

2. An Indirect Question includes all the cases where an interrogative clause, or one introduced by an interrogative word (*who? where? whether*, and the like) is made the subject or object of a verb or of some equivalent phrase. As most interrogatives, both in English and Latin, have the same form with the relatives, care must be taken to distinguish them by noticing whether there is an Antecedent, expressed or implied, which is the distinguishing mark of the Relative.

N. B. For other interrogative forms see § **71.**

Exercise 29.

1. When I came to the foot of the hill, I met with a very aged man, who asked me what I was and whither bound. I told him that I was a pilgrim going to the celestial city. Then said the old man, " Thou lookest like an honest fellow. Wilt thou be content to dwell with me for the wages that I shall give thee? " Then I asked him his name, and where he dwelt. He said his name was Adam the first, and that he dwelt in the town of Deceit. I asked him then what was his work, and what the wages that he would give. He told me that his work was many delights, and his wages, that I should be his heir at last.

2. His resolution was immediately formed. He rose and called together the officers of Proxenus, and addressed them. After[1] having pointed out the magnitude of the evils which they had to apprehend, unless some provision were made without delay for their defence, he dexterously turned their attention to

---

[1] *cum.*

a more animating view of the situation. "Ever since they had concluded the treaty with Tissaphernes, he had observed with envy and regret the rich possessions of the barbarians, and had lamented that his comrades had bound themselves to abstain from the good things which they saw within their reach, except [1] so far as they were able to purchase a taste [2] of them at an [3] expense which he had feared would soon exhaust their scanty means."

3. I fancy, Cephalus, that people do not generally acquiesce in these views of yours, because they think that it is not your character but your great wealth that enables you to bear with old age. For the rich, it is said, have many consolations. "True," he said, " they will not believe me; and they are partly right, though not so right as they suppose. There is great truth in the reply of Themistocles to the Seriphian, who tauntingly told him that his reputation was due not to himself but to his country. ' I should not have become famous if I had been a native of Seriphus, neither would you if [you had been] an Athenian.' "

4. I will tell you [a tale of] what happened once to a brave man, Er, son of Armenius, a native of Pamphylia. His story was,[4] that when the soul had gone out of him, it travelled in company with many others, till they came to a mysterious place, in which were two gaps adjoining one another in the earth, and exactly opposite them two gaps above in the heaven. Between these gaps sat judges, who, after passing sentence, commanded the just to take the road to the right, upwards through the heaven; while the unjust were ordered to take the road downwards, to the left.

---

[1] *praeterquam quae.*   [2] *pauca.*   [3] *tantus.*
[4] *dico.*

Lesson 31.

Certain Special Constructions.

1. READ carefully §§ **70,** 4. *c*, and **57,** 8. *g* (Exclamatory clauses) ; **70,** 4. *d* ("so far from" &c.) ; **70,** 4. *e*, comparing **58,** 11. *f* (**facere ut**) ; **70,** 4. *g*, and **65,** 1. *a, b* (**quin, quominus**) ; **72,** 3. *b* (Participle with **habeo**) ; **64,** 1. *b*, with Remark (disguised Purpose) ; **71,** 2. with *a, b, d* (Double Questions) ; **59,** 3. *d, e, f ;* 4. *d ;* '09 2. *c* (Indicative in conditions for Subjunctive).

2. Some constructions which belong logically under the preceding heads have special idiomatic uses in Latin. Such are the following : —

a. The English exclamations, "The idea that!" "To think that!" "That!" and the like, referring to *something which has actually happened*, are expressed by the Accusative and Infinitive, usually with the enclitic **ne.** When referring to *something anticipated* or to *a mere idea*, by **ut** with the subjunctive, usually also with -**ne** : as,

1. **To think that you should have fallen into such grief for me !** *te in tantas aerumnas propter me incidisse !*
2. **What! I interrupt you?** *egone ut te interpellem ?*

b. English expressions, like "Far from," or "So far from," with a following clause, are rendered in Latin by **tantum abest,** followed by two clauses with **ut.** The former clause is always the subject of **abest,** which has not a personal subject, as in English ; the latter clause is always one of Result, not an independent clause, as it often is in English (see examples in Grammar).

c. Such phrases as "To allow one's self to," "manage to," "act in any way in doing a thing," are expressed in Latin by **facere** or **committere,** with an ut-clause as object. So also where verbs want the future infinitive, **fore** (**futurum esse**) **ut** is used.

d. Expressions implying Hindrance, usually (but not always) followed in English by FROM with the participial noun, take in Latin a subjunctive clause with **quominus** (rarely **ne**). If the hindering is NEGATIVED, **quin** may be used instead. The same construction is used in Latin with verbs of *refusing*. Expressions like "Not to doubt THAT (*but that*)" are regularly followed by **quin**. The accusative with infinitive is to be avoided. "To doubt whether," introduces an Indirect Question, and is so to be treated. "To hesitate" is expressed by the same verb (**dubito**), but with a different construction — the simple Infinitive.

e. The English HAVE, with a participle, is sometimes a mere auxiliary, corresponding to the Perfect in Latin. Sometimes, however, it retains a slight notion of *possession*, and is then to be translated literally, with **habeo** or **teneo**. Thus —

1. **I have guarded the prisoners,** *captivos custodii.* But —
2. **I have the prisoners guarded (under guard),** *captivos habeo custoditos.*

f. Parenthetical expressions, like "To be brief," "To say no more," "So to speak," are really expressions of Purpose, and are to be so treated in Latin : as,

Not to be tedious, the enemy were beaten and put to flight, *ne longus sim, hostes pulsi et fugati sunt.*

N. B. As this expression is elliptical, the sequence of tenses is disregarded.

g. For the treatment of Double or Alternative Questions, consult the forms in the Grammar (§ **71**, 2).

h. In stating the *propriety*, *possibility*, and the like, of a future action, or one that has not been performed at all, Latin employs the Indicative, expressing it (as it were) as a general truth, where English uses the Potential, treating it as a particular case. For example —

1. **It would be tedious to follow up the matter,** *longum est rem persequi.*
2. **It would befit us to mourn (but we do not),** *nos decebat lugere.*
3. **How much better would it have been!** *Quanto melius fuerat!*

Exercise 30.

1. I do not doubt that you fully agree with me regarding the motives and the consequences of Cæsar's murder. I, for my part, cannot avoid feeling both sorrow and indignation, whether [1] I consider the victim or [1] the assassins in that great crime. Whatever may have been the ambitions or the vices of his earlier public or private life, they cannot prevent us from regarding his death at this time as the most serious calamity to the Roman people, or from condemning and execrating the infamous conspiracy that slew him. Not to speak of the glory and empire won to Rome by his victories, he was the first conqueror in civil war who refused to make it an occasion of massacre and revenge. Far from following the example of violence which the partisans of Pompey had threatened, he had [2] disciplined and controlled his forces, so as effectually to check the fury of slaughter or the lust of plunder. At least, his mercy to his enemies, after the victory at Pharsalia, should have [3] forbidden all thoughts of private resentment. [To think] that Marcus Brutus, whom he not only had spared on the field of battle and in the hostile camp, but even called his son, should strike the deadliest blow against him! that Cicero, who had so lately extolled with fulsome praise [4] his pardon [5] of Marcellus, should with yet greater fervor have gloried in the manner of his death! Was it the hope of real liberty, or was it jealousy of his more vigorous genius and more dazzling glory?

---

[1] *sive.* [2] *habeo.* [3] *debuerat.*
[4] *effusis laudibus efferre.* [5] Clause with **quod.**

2. But the death of Cæsar could not cause [1] true and lasting freedom to exist in a city which had beheld the murder of Gracchus, the massacres of Marius, the proscriptions of Sulla, the profligacy of Catiline, the violence of Clodius! The wicked act [2] of his enemies did not hinder Rome from becoming subject to the tyranny of a Cæsar; it did prevent it from enjoying a firm peace and an enlightened rule under the ancient forms of the commonwealth. It kindled again the fury of civil war. It destroyed the remnant of those ancient families and the authority of the Senate, which had made the glory of Rome. It extinguished the freedom of debate, and all confidence among men. It committed the destiny of the Republic to the hands of Mark Antony and Octavianus. It removed the mighty Julius, to prepare the way for Tiberius, Caligula, and Nero.

[1] Lit. " bring it to pass that," &c.   [2] *facinus.*

VOCABULARY.

A.

A, an, usually omitted ; a certain, *quidam.*
abandon, *relinquo, amitto.*[3]
abide, *maneo,*[2] *mansi.*
abode, to make, *habito.*[1] [*circa.*
about (here and there), *passim ;*
above, *supra* (acc.), *insuper* ; above all, *maxime.*
abroad, to get, *emano.*[1]
abstain, *tempero.*[1]
abundance, *abundantia, ae.*
abundant, *satis* (with gen.).
abuse (v.), *abutor,*[3] *usus.*
academy, *academia, ae.*
accept, *accipio,*[3] *cepi.*
accompany, *comitor.*[1]
account (v.), *habeo,*[2] *existimo.*[1]
account, on — of, *ob, propter* (acc.) ; it is of — , *interest* (see § **50,** 4. *d*). (See p. 29).

accuse, *accuso.*[1]
accustomed, to be, *soleo,*[2] *solitus.*
achieve, *gero,*[3] *gessi.*
acquiesce, *consentior,*[4] *sensus.*
Acron, *Acron, onis.*
across, *trans* (acc.).
act (n.), *factum, i.*
act as, *se gerere ;* —a part, *partes agere, tueri.*
acting, *actio in scena.*
actor, *actor, oris.*
Adam, *Adamus, i.*
add, *addo.*[3]
addition of territory, *fines promoti.*
adjoining, *conjunctus.*
address, *adloquor,*[3] *appello.*[1]
admire, *miror.*[1]
advance, *progredior,*[3] *gressus.*
advantage, *utilitas, atis ;* I have the — of, *me adjuvat quod.*
advise, *hortor,*[1] *moneo.*[2]

affair, *res, rei* (F.).

affections, *animi, orum.*

afflicted, *adflictus.*

afraid, to be, *timeo,*[2] *ui.*

after, *post.*

afterwards, *postea.*

again, *iterum, rursus, postea.*

against, *contra, adversus* (acc.).

Agamemnon, *Agamemnon, ŏnis,* acc. *ŏna.*

age, *aetas, atis* (F.).

aged, *confectus (provectus) ae-tate, longaevus.*

agitate, *commoveo,*[2] *movi.*

ago, *abhinc.*

agree, *adsentior*[4] (dat.).

agreeable, *gratus, a, um.*

aid, *auxilium, i.*

air (music), *cantus, ūs.*

alarm, *terreo,*[2] *ui.*

alarmed, *territus* (abl.), *sollici-tus;* — for, *metuens* (dat.).

alas, *vae!*

Alcibiades, *Alcibiades, is.*

all, *omnis, e* (whole), *totus, solus* (gen. *ius*).

all in a body, *universi.*

allied, *conjunctus.*

allot, *tribuo,*[3] *ui, utum.*

allow, *potestatem dare* (dat.).

ally, *socius, i.*

almost, *fere, paene.*

along, *praeter.* — alone, *solus.*

along with, *una cum.*

already, *jam.*

also, *quoque.*

altar, *ara, ae.*

although, *quanquam.*

altogether, *omnino.*

always, *semper.*

ambassador, *legatus, i.*

ambition, *ambitio, onis; cupid-itas, atis* (F.).

ambitious, *ambitiosus.*

among, *inter* (acc.) ; sometimes expressed by dat. ; *apud.*

ancestor, *proavus, i, auctor generis;* pl., *majores, um.*

ancient, *antiquus, vetus, eris.*

and, *et, -que* (enclitic), *atque.*

anger, *ira* (visit with, *persequi*).

animal (wild), *fera, ae* (F.) ; the lower animals, *bestiae.*

animating, *laetus.*

answer, *respondeo,*[2] *di, sum.*

annual, *annuus, sollemnis.*

Antipater, *Antipater, tris.*

antiquities, *antiquitas, atis* (F.).

anxiety, *sollicitudo, inis* (F.).

anxious, *sollicitus.*

any, *ullus, ullo modo;* — one, *quisquam, quivis* (p. 18) ; does any ? *num quis ?*

Apennines, *Apenninus* (sc. *mons*), *i* (M.).

apparel, *vestitus, ūs;* in funeral —, *sordide vestitus.*

appear, *appareo,*[2] *ui; videor.*[2]

appease, *lenio,*[4] *placo.*[1]

apply (for aid), *se conferre, peto.*

apprehend, *metuo.*[3]

apprise, *doceo.*[2]

appoint, *praeficio* (gen.).

appointed (to head), *praefec-tus datus.*

approach (n.), *adventus, ūs.*

approval, *gratia, ae.*

arbitration, *arbitrium, i.*

arbitrator, *arbiter, tri.*

archbishop, *archiepiscopus, i.*

arduous, *arduus.*

Argos, *Argi, orum.*

aristocracy, *nobilitas, atis.*

arm (v.), *armo.*[1]

armed, *armatus.*

arms (weapons), *arma, orum.*

army, *exercitus, ūs.*

arrival, *adventus, ūs.*

arrive, *pervenio,*[4] *advenio.*[4]

arrogance, *arrogantia, ae.*

arrow, *sagitta, ae.*

art, *ars, tis* (F.).

artificial, *artificiosus.*

artisan, *opifex, icis.*

Aruns, *Aruns, Aruntis.*

as, *ut;* (when), *cum.*

as . . as, *tam . . quam.*

as if, as it were, *tanquam.*

ascent, *ascensus, ūs.*

ashamed, to be, *pudere* (impers. § 50, 4. *c*).

aside, *se-* (verb-prefix).

ask, *rogo,*[3] *quaero*[3] *sibi* (*ab*).

assassin, *sicarius, i.*

assassinate, *interficio,*[3] *occido.*[3]

assistance, *auxilium, i.*

assume, *sumo,*[3] *adrogo.*[1]

assumed, *simulatus.*

Assyrian, *Assyrius.*

at, with name of town, locative ; near (not in), *apud, ad;* as cause (as "alarmed at"), abl. ; at all, *omnino;* at once, *statim.*

Athenian, *Atheniensis, e.*

Athens, *Athenae, arum.*

attached to, *conjunctus cum.*

attack, *aggredior,*[3] *gressus.*

attain, *adsequor.*[3]

attempt (v.), *conor.*[1]

attempt (n.), *conatus, ūs* (M.).

attend, *comitor;*[1] to — the session of the Senate, *in Senātum ire.*

attendant, *socius, i.*

attention, to pay, *specto;*[1] to turn, *animum revocare.*

attitude, *status, ūs.*

attractive, *jucundus.*

audacious, *audax, acis.*

augury, *augurium, i.*

authority, *auctoritas, atis* (F.).

avenge, *ulciscor,*[3] *ultus.*

avert, *averto, ti, sum.*[3]

avoid, *fugio,*[3] *fugi, evito;*[1] I cannot — , *non possum non.*

await, *exspecto.*[1]

awake, *e somno excitare.*

aware, to be, *animadvertere.*

away, to be, *abesse.*

awhile, *aliquamdiu.*

axe, *securis, is* (F.).

B.

babe, *infans, tis.*

banish, *pello,*[3] *pepuli, pulsum;* *expello.*[2]

bank, *ripa, ae.*

bar (v.), *claudo,*[3] *di, sum.*

barbarian, *barbarus.*

barbarously, *saeviter.*

barren - of, to be, *careo,*[2] *ui* (abl.).

battle, *proelium, i* (N.); *pugna, ae* (F.) ; field of battle, *acies, ei* (F.), *locus ubi pugnatur.*

bay, *sinus, ūs.*

be, *sum* (see paradigms of compound tense) ; to be so, *ita se habere;* — able *posse.*

beach, *litus, ŏris* (N.).

bear, *fero, ferre, tuli, latum.*

bear up, *sustineo,*[2] *ui.*

bear no relation to, *nihil attinere ad.*

beard, *barba, ae.*

beast, wild, *fera, ae.*

beating, *vis, vis* (F.).

beautiful, *pulcher, a, um.*

beauty, *species, ei, forma, ae.*

because, *quia.*

become, *fio, fieri* (or passive).

before, *ante, antehac, antequam.*

begin, *incipio,[3] cepi; coepi.*

beginning, *initium, i.*

behalf, in, *pro* (abl.).

behave, *se gerere.*

behind, *post;* go behind, *sequor.[3]*

behold, *contueor, video, conspicio.*

believe, *credo [3]* (dat.).

belong, *esse* (with gen. or dat.); *pertineo,[1] ui (ad).*

bench, *subsellium, i.*

beneath, *subter.*

beneficent, *beneficus* (use superl.).

beneficial, *utilis, e.*

besides, *praeter, praeterea.*

besiege, *oppugno.[1]*

besiegers, *obsidentes.*

best, *optimus;* (adv.) *optime, maxime;* (of two) *magis.*

bestow, *dono.[1]*

betray, *prodo,[3] ostendo.[3]*

better, *melior, us.*

between, *inter* (acc.).

bid, *jubeo,[2] jussi.*

bind, *obligo.[1]*

bird, *avis, is* (F.).

birth, by, *natu.*

bite, *mordeo,[2] momordi.*

bitter, *acerbus.*

bitterly, *vehementer.*

blame, *culpa, ae.*

bland, *blandus.*

blast, of music, *clangor, oris* (M.).

blow (a blast of an instrument), *edo.[3]*

blow, *ictus, ūs* (M.); *plaga, ae* (F.), *vulnus, eris* (N.).

boar, *aper, apri.*

boast, *glorior,[1] praedico [1] de.*

bodily gifts, *bona corporis.*

body, *corpus, oris* (N.); of men, *agmen, inis* (N.).

bolster-up, *subvenio [4]* (dat.).

bondage, *servitus, utis* (F.).

book, *liber, bri* (M.).

booty, *praeda, ae.*

borders, *fines, ium* (M.).

born, *natus;* to be — , *nascor.[3]*

both, *uterque, utraque, utrumque,* gen. *utriusque;* both . . and, *et . . et.*

bound, *obligatus;* to be going anywhere, *tendere.*

bow one's head, *se inclinare.*

boy, *puer, eri.*

brave, *fortis, e.*

break, *frango,[3] fregi, fractum.*

break up, *confringo.*

breathe, *exspiro;[1] animam efflare,* to breathe one's last.

breathing, *spiritum ducens.*

breeze, *aura, ae.*

bribe (v.), *corrumpo,[3] rupi, ruptum.*

bribes (n.), *dona, orum.*

bribery, *ambitus, ūs* (M.).

bridge, *pons, pontis* (M.).

bright, *clarus;* — distinctions, *praeclara.*

brilliant, *clarus, insignis, e, splendidus.*

bring, *adfero,* irr., *porto,*[1] *duco, perduco ;*[3] — to an end, *conficio ;*[3] — to pass, *efficio.*[3]

broken, *fractus, turbatus.*

brother, *frater, tris* (M.) ; — in-law, *uxoris frater.*

brutality, *immanitas, atis* (F.).

brute, *bestia, ae* (F.).

build, *aedifico ;*[1] military works, roads, &c., *munio.*[4]

building, *aedificium, i.*

bulk, *magnitudo, inis* (F.).

bull, *taurus, i.*

burn (v.), *ardeo,*[2] *si.*

burst, *inrumpo.*[3]

business, *negotium ;* make it one's —, *operam ponere in.*

but, *sed, autem* (§ **43**, 3. *b*), *tamen ;* but if, *sin, quod si ;* —

buy, *emo.*[3] [for, *nisi* (with verb).

by (near), *ad ;* (with passives) *ab, a* (abl.) ; means, ablative alone (see p. 28) ; by far, *longe ;* be by (near), *adesse.*

C.

Cadiz, *Gades, ium* (F.).

Cæsar, *Caesar, äris ;* adj., *Caesarianus.*

Caenina (of), *Caeninensis, e.*

calamity, *calamitas, atis* (F.).

call, *appello,*[1] *advoco ;*[1] — to mind, *commemorare ;*[1] — upon (for opinion), *sententiam rogare ;* — together, *convoco.*

camp, *castra, orum* (N.) ; of the camp, *militaris, e.*

campaign, *bellum, i.*

can, *possum, posse, potui.*

candidate, to become (for consul), *consulatum petere.*

cap, *pileus, i* (M.).

capitol, *capitolium, i.*

captain, *dux, ducis.*

captivated, *captus.*

capture (v.), *capio.*[3]

capture, *expugnatio, onis* (F.).

care, *cura, ae.*

careful of, *studiosus* (gen.).

carry, *porto,*[1] *fero, deicio.*[3]

Carthage, *Carthago, inis* (F.).

Carthaginian, *Carthaginiensis.*

cast, *proicio ;*[3] — the parts of a play, *distribuo.*

cast, *jactus* (part. of *jacio*).

cat, *felis, is.*

catch, *excipio ;*[3] — at, *capto.*[1]

Catiline, *Catilina, ae.*

Cato, *Cato, onis.*

Caudine Forks, *Furcae Caudinae.*

cause to suffer, *aliqua re adficere ; efficere ut.*

cause, *res, rei ; causa, ae ; res* (plur.).

cavalier, *eques, itis.*

cavalry, *eques, itis,* pl.

celebrate, *celebro.*[1]

celestial, *caelestis, e.*

censor, *censor, oris ;* one who has been —, *censorius, i.*

censure, *reprehendo.*[3]

chain, *vinculum, i.*

chair, *sella, ae* (F.).

champion, *defensor, oris.*

chance, *occasio oblata ; casus, ūs* (M.) ; by chance, *forte.*

change, *muto.*[1]

character, *indoles, is* (F.).
charge, *accusatio, onis* (F.).
Charles, *Carolus, i.*
chariot, *currus, ūs* (M.).
chase, *venatio, onis* (F.).
chastise, *verbero.*[1]
check, *reprimo.*[3]
cheer, *recreo.*[1]
cherish, *gero,*[3] *gessi.*
chief, *dux, cis ; princeps, ipis.*
chief-town, *caput gentis.*
chiefly, *maxime.*
child, *puer, i ;* adj. *puerilis, e.*
children, *liberi ;* young —, *pueri, orum, infantes.*
childless, *orbus.*
chink, *rima, ae.*
choose, *delego,*[3] *gi ;* (of officers) *facio,*[3] *feci ; creo.*[1]
Cicero, *Cicero, onis.*
circle, *circulus ;* (v.) *circa esse.*
circumstance, *res, rei.*
citizen, *civis, is.*
city, *urbs, urbis, civitas, atis* (F.) ; of the —, *urbanus.*
civil, *civilis, e.*
claim, *vindico.*[1]
class, *ordo, inis* (M.).
claw, *unguis, is* (M.).
cleft, *fissus* (part. of *findo*).
clemency, *clementia, ae.*
client, *cliens, tis.*
climb, *scando,*[3] *adscendo.*[3]
close (v.), *claudo,*[3] *si, sum.*
close to, *prope a* (abl.).
closed, *clausus.*
clothed, *vestitus.*
coast, *litus, ŏris* (N.).
coil, *volvo.*[3]
cold, *algor, oris* (M.).
colleague, *collega, ae.*

college, *collegium, i.*
colony, *colonia, ae.*
come, *venio,*[4] *veni ;* — across, *transeo, ire ;* — forward, *exsisto ;* [3] — in (of wind), *adflare ;* — to, *pervenio* [4] *ad, accedo* [3] *ad.*
comeliness, *forma, ae.*
command (v.), *jubeo,*[2] *jussi ;* (in office), *praeesse ;* be master of, *impero.*[2]
command (n.), *imperatum, i ;* supreme —, *imperium, i ;* by —, *jussu.*
commander, *imperator, oris.*
commanding, *dux, ducis* (gen.) ; as descriptive adj., *augustus.*
commend, *laudo.*[1] [*committo.*
commit (an act), *facio, efficio,*[3]
common (in common), *communis, e.*
common people, *plebs, is* (F.).
commonwealth, *res publica.*
communicate, *impertio.*[4]
community, *populus, i.*
companion, *socius, i.*
compare, *comparo.*[1]
company : in — with, *una cum.*
complete, *ad finem perduco.*[3]
completely, *plane.*
compelled, *coactus* (*cogo*).
compose, *concipio, scribo.*[3]
compulsion, under, *coactus.*
comrade, *comes, itis.*
conceal, *celo* [2] (two acc.), *occulo.*[2]
concerns, it, *refert* (§ **40**, 4. *d*).
conclude (make), *facio.*[2]
condemn, *damno,*[1] *reprehendo.*[3]
condition, *condicio fortunae ; fortunae, arum.*
conduct (v.), *duco,*[3] *deduco.*[3]

Vocabulary.

conduct (n.), *facta, orum.*

confederation, *foedus, eris* (N.).

confer on, *defero ad, confero in.*

confidence, *fiducia, ae, fides.*

confidence, to have — in, *confido* [3] (dat.).   [*obsecro.*

conical, *coni* (gen.). — conjure,

connect, *conjungo.*[3]

connected, *conjunctus.*

conquer, *vinco,*[3] *vici, victum;* *devinco.*

conqueror, *victor, oris.*

consequences, *exitus, ūs* (sing.).

consider, *existimo,*[1] *considero.*[1]

consideration, *res, rei* (F.).

consistent, to be, *congruo.*[3]

consolation, *solatio, consolatio, onis* (F.).

conspicuous, to be, *emineo.*[2]

conspiracy, *conjuratio, onis.*

conspirator, *conjurator, oris.*

conspire, *conjuro.*[1]

consul, *consul, ulis;* (one who has been), *consularis.*

consulship, *consulatus, ūs* (M.); in one's consulship, *consul,* in appos. with name.

consult, *consulo,*[3] *ui* (§ **51**, 2. *a* [3]).

consume, *consumo.*[3]

contempt (with), *fastidiens, tis.*

contend (as with difficulty), *laboro* [1] (abl.).

content, contented, *contentus* (abl.); wilt thou be —, *satin habes?*

continue, *persequor,*[3] *secutus;* — in pursuit, *hostes consectari.*

contrary to, *contra* (acc.).

control, *moderatio, onis* (F.).

controlled, *frenatus.*

convict, *convinco,*[3] *damno.*[1]

corner, *angulus, i.*

counsellor, to have, *in consilium adhibere.*

count (a title of rank), *comes, itis.*

countless, *innumerabilis, e.*

country, *regio, onis; terra, ae;* (one's native), *patria, ae;* — people, *agrestes, ium, rustici, orum;* in the —, *ruri.*

court, *aula, ae.*

covered, *tectus* (F.) *coopertus;* (here and there, as with dwellings), *sparsus.*

cowardice, *ignavia, ae.*

cowardly, *ignavus.*

cradle, *arca, ae.*

crafty, *dolosus.*

crawl, *serpo.*[3]

create, *creo;* [1] *facio,*[3] *feci;* *constituo.*[3]

credit (v.), *confido.*[3]

credit (n.), *laus, dis* (F.).

Creon, *Creon, ontis.*

crime, *scelus, eris* (N.).

crisis, *discrimen, inis* (N.).

cross, *transire.*

crowd, *comitatus, ūs, turba, ae.*

crown, *corona, ae;* (royal power), *imperium.*

cruel, *crudelis, e.*

cry, *clamo;* [1] — out, *clamo, exclamo.*[1]

cultivated, *cultus.*

curious, *memorabilis, e.*

curule, *curulis, e.*

custom, *mos, moris* (M.).

cynic, *cynicus.*

D.

danger, *periculum, i.*
dangerous, *gravis, e.*
daughter, *filia, ae.*
day, *dies, diei* (M.), (rarely F. in singular).
dazzling, *clarus.*
dead (slain), *occisus.*
deadliest, *gravissimus.*
dearly, *care, carissime.*
death, *mors, tis;* condemn to —, *damnare capitis* (§ 50, 4. *b*), *morte multare;* put to —, *interficere.*
debar, *prohibeo,*[2] *ui, itum.*
debase, *depravo.*[1]
debate, *sententias dicere.*
debt (kindness), *beneficium, i.*
deceit, *fallacia, ae.*
deceive, *decipio.*[3]
decemvir, *decemvir, viri.*
decide the contest, *decerto.*[1]
decision, *judicium, i.*
declare, *nuntio,*[1] *adfirmo.*[1]
dedicate, *dedico.*[1]
deed, *factum, i.*
deem, *puto.*[1]
deeply, *vehementer.*
defeat (v.), *supero.*[1]
defeat (n.), *calamitas, clades.*
defend, *defendo;* defence, *salus.*
degree (to what —), *quo.*
delay, *mora, ae.*
deliberate, *delibero.*[1]
delight (v.), *delecto.*[1]
delight (n.), *gaudium, i; delectatio, onis* (F.); *oblectamentum, i.*
deliver, *libero,*[1] *trado.*[3]
deliverer, *liberator, oris.*

demand, *postulo,*[1] *flagito.*[1]
Demosthenes, *Demosthenes, is.*
deny, *nego.*[1]
depose (a king), *regno spolio.*[1]
deprive, *orbo,*[1] *privo;*[1] — of voice, *vocem eripere* (dat.).
deputation, *legatio, onis* (F.).
descended, *genitus* (with abl.).
descend, *descendo.*[3]
descent, *genus, eris* (N.).
desert (n.), *deserta, orum.*
deserted, *desertus.*
desire, *cupio,*[3] *ivi* (with acc. or infin.), *jubeo.*[2]
desire (n.), *cupido, inis* (F.).
despatch, *conficio,*[3] *interficio.*[3]
despise, *contemno,*[3] *psi.*
despoil, *spolio.*[2]
despotism, *dominatio, onis* (F.).
destiny, *fortuna, ae.*
destroy, *deleo,*[2] *evi, etum.*
destroyer, *perditor, oris.*
destruction, *exitium, i.*
detected, *detectus.*
determine, *statuo;*[3] — on, *capere.*
detestable, *nefandus.*
devoid, *expers, tis* (with gen.).
devotions (of —), *precandi* (gen.).
dexterously, *dextre.*
diadem, *diadema, atis* (N.).
dictator, *dictator, oris.*
dictatorship, *dictatura, ae.*
die, *morior,*[3] *mortuus.*
die out, *exstinguor.*[3]
die (n.), *alea, ae.*
dignity, *dignitas, atis* (F.).
difficult, *difficilis, e.*
dinner, *cena, ae* (F.).
dip, *tingo,*[3] *tinxi, tinctum.*

direct, *viam monstrare.*
disappear, *evanesco,*[3] *ui.*
disaster, *clades, is* (F.).
discharge, *praesto,*[1] *stiti.*
disciplined, *coercitus.*
discontinue, *abrogo.*[1]
discourse (v.), *disputo.*[1]
discovery (conduct to —), *efficere ut inveniret.*
discredit, *infamia, ae* (F.).
disease, *morbus, i* (M.).
disgrace, *ignominia, dedecus.*
display, *praebeo.*[2]
dispirited, *fractus animo.*
displease, *displiceo, ui* (dat.).
disposer, *rector et moderator.*
disposition, *voluntas, atis.*
disregard, *neglego, xi.*
dissatisfied, *non contentus.*
dissembler, *simulator, oris.*
dissolution, *solutio, onis* (F.).
distinguish, *laudibus ornare;* with distinction, *honorifice.*
distress, *res adversae.*
distribute, *distribuo.*[3]
distrust, *diffidentia, ae.*
disunion, *dissensio, onis* (F.).
divide, *divido,*[3] *si, sum.*
divine, *divinus.*
diviner, *haruspex, icis.*
divinity, *natura divina.*
do, *facio,*[3] *feci, factum.*
dog, *canis, is* (gen. pl. *canum*).
dominion (subjects), *civitas, atis* (F.).
doom: to seal —, *pernicies atque exitium esse.*
door, *fores, ium* (F.); *porta, ae* (F.); out of doors, *foras.*
doubtful, *dubius.*
downward, *deorsum.*

drama, *fabula, ae.*
draw up, *subduco;*[3] troops —, *copias instruo.*[3]
drink (n.), *potio, onis* (F.).
drive, *pello,*[3] *pepuli, pulsum.*
drowned: to be —, *mortuus esse submersus.*
dry, *siccus.*
dry (up), *exsicco.*[2]
due, to be, *deberi.*
duly, *rite.*
duty, *munus, eris; officium, i.*
dwell, habito.[1]

E.

eagerness, earnestness, *studium, i;* eagerly, *avide.*
eagle, *aquila, ae.*
earlier, *prior, oris.*
early, *mane.*
early-ripe, *maturus.*
earnest: in —, *serio.*
earth, *terra, ae;* surface of — expressed by *omnis.*
ease, *tranquillitas, atis* (F.).
East, *oriens, tis* (M.); of the —, *Asiaticus.*
easy, *facilis, e.*
educate, *educo.*[1]
education, *disciplina, ae.*
effectually, *penitus.*
effeminacy, *mollities, ei* (F.).
effort, to make, *nitor.*[3]
Egypt, *Aegyptus, i* (F.).
elder, *major* (*natu*).
elect, *creo;*[1] *facio,*[3] *feci, factus.*
election (as consul), *consulatus, us* (M.).
elegy, *elegia, ae.*

elephant, *elephantus, i.*
eloquence, *eloquentia, ae.*
emblem, *signum, i.*
eminent, *illustris, e.*
empire, *imperium, i.*
employ, *utor,*[8] *usus.*
empty, *inanis, e.*
enable, *facere ut possim.*
encounter (v.), *confligo*[8] *cum.*
encourage, *cohortor.*[1]
end (v.), *finio.*[4]
end, *finis, is* (M.) ; at an —,
    finitus; bring to an —, *confi-
    cio,*[3] *feci ;* — of, *extremus.*
endanger, *in periculum addu-
    cere.*
endless, *sine fine.*
endowed, *praeditus.*
endure, *fero (perfero), tuli;* ca-
    pable of enduring, *patiens, tis.*
enemy, *hostis, is* (" the enemy,"
    usually plur.) ; a personal —,
    inimicus, i.
energy, *studium, i.*
engage, *adhibeo,*[2] *ui, itum.*
engage in, *inire.*
engaged, *occupatus.*
English, *Angli, orum.*
enjoy (fruit), *percipio.*[3]
enlightened rule, *imperium sa-
    pienter administratum.*
enmity, *odium, i.*
Enna (man of), *Hennensis, is.*
enrich, *locupleto.*[1]
ensign, *insigne, is* (N.).
enter, *intro;*[1] *ineo, ire;* —a
    ship, *conscendo.*[3]
enterprise, *conatus, ūs* (M.).
entire, *totus* (gen. *ius*).
entitle, *inscribo.*[3]
entreat, *obsecro.*[1]

envenomed, *venenatus.*
envy, *invideo ; invidia.*
Epidaurian, *Epidaurius.*
Epirots, *Epirotae, arum.*
equal, *par, paris.*
equally, *non minus.*
establish, *conloco.*[1]
estate, *praedium, i.*
esteem (v.), *aestimo.*[1]
Etruscan, *Etruscus.*
even, *etiam ;* not —, *ne . . qui-
    dem ;* —as, *ut.*
event, *factum, i; eventus, ūs*
    (M.).
ever, *unquam ;* (always), *semper.*
every, everybody, *quisque, qui-
    libet, omnis, unusquisque* (p.
    19).
everywhere, *ubique, ubivis.*
evil, *malus;* (n.),*incommodum, i.*
exactly, *plane.*
exalted, *excelsus.*
example, *exemplum, i.*
except, *praeter* (acc.), *nisi.*
excess, *nimium.—* excel, *excello.*
excited, *concitatus.*
exclaim, *clamo.*[1]
execrate, *exsecror.*[1]
exercise (v.), *exerceo,*[2] *ui, itum.*
exercise (n.), *exercitatio, onis*
    (use plur.).
exert, *exerceo,*[2] *ui.*
exertion, *labor, oris* (M.).
exhaust, *conficio,*[3] *exhaurio.*[4]
exigency, *necessitas, atis* (F.).
exile, *exsilium, i;* to be in —,
    exsulo ;[1] an —, *exsul, ŭlis.*
expel, *expello,*[3] *puli, pulsum.*
expense, *pretium, i.*
experience (v.), *obire* (acc.).
exploit, *res gesta.*

expose, *obicio,*[3] *jeci ; offero.*
exterminate, *exstirpo.*[1]
extinguish, *restinguo,*[3] *nxi.*
extirpate, *exstirpo.*[1]
extort, *extorqueo,*[2] *torsi.*
extraordinary, *extraordinarius.*
extremely, express by superl.
eye, *oculus, i* (M.).

F.

face, *vultus, ūs* (M.).
facilitate, *adjuvo,*[1] *juvi.*
failings, *vitia, orum.*
fair share, *justa pars.*
fair speaking, *blandiloquus.*
faith : on the — of, *fretus* (with abl.).
faithful, *fidus.*
Falerian, *Falerius.*
fall, *cado,*[3] *pereo ;* — to the lot of, *obtingo, tigi* (of office, use rather *obtinere,* of the man chosen) ; let —, *deicio ;* — in with, *occurro ;*[3] — upon, *invadere in ;* — down, *decido ;*[3] — on one's knees, *in genua procumbere.*
false, *falsus.*
faltering, *vacillans, tis.*
fame, *fama, ae.*
family, *familia, ae.*
famine, *fames, is* (F.).
famous, *clarus.*
fancy, *opinor.*[1]   [*late.*
far, by far, *longe ;* far and wide,
farewell, *vale.*
fate, *fatum, i ; Fortuna, ae.*
father, *pater, tris ; parens, tis ;* of the fathers, *patrius.*

fatigue, *labor, oris* (M.).
fault, *culpa, ae.*
favor (v.), *faveo,*[2] *favi, fautum.*
favor (n.), *beneficium, i.*
favorable, *secundus ;* prove —, *bene succedere.*
fear (v.), *timeo,*[2] *metuo,*[3] *vereor.*[2]
fear (n.), *timor, oris ; metus, ūs.*
feeble, *exiguus.*
feel, *sentio,*[4] *sensi ; adficior* (with abl.).
fellow, *vir, viri.*
ferment, *agitatio, onis* (F.).
fervor, *studium, i.*
festival, *festus dies.*
few, *aliquot, pauci, ae, a.*
field, *ager, gri* (M.), *arvum, i.*
fierce, *acer, ferox ;* fiercely disputed victory, *acerrimis pugnis parta.*
fig, *ficus, ūs* (F.).
fig-tree, *ficus, i* (F.).
fight (v.), *pugno ;* — a battle, *committo.*[3]
fight (n.), *pugna, ae.*
figure, *species, ei* (F.), *statura.*
fill, *compleo, impleo.*[2]
find, *invenio,*[4] *video.*[2]
finish, *perago.*[3]
fire, *ignis, is* (M.).
firm, *firmus.*
first, *primus ;* at —, *primo ;* (beforehand), *ante.*
fitting, to be, *decere.*
fix, *figo.*[3]
flame, *flamma, ae* (F.), *ignis, is* (M.).
flee, *fugio,*[3] *fugi ; confugio.*
fleet, *classis, is* (F.).
flight, *fuga, ae.*
flock, *pecus, oris* (N.).

flog, *fustibus caedere.*
flow, *fluo,*[3] *xi, xum.*
foe, *hostis, is* (M.).
fold, *sinus, ūs* (M.).
follow, *sequor,*[3] *insequor, imitor.*
follower, *comes, itis.*
food, *cibus, i* (M.). — foot, *pes.*
foot, of hill, *imus collis;* — (infantry), *pedes, itis* (pl.).
for (prep.), *pro* (abl.) ; often expressed by dative (§ **51,** 7. R.).
for, *nam, enim, etenim* (§ **43,** 3. *d*) ; (instead of), *in loco.*
forbid, *veto,*[1] *ui.*
forces, *copiae, arum.*
forest, *silva, ae.*
forfend: heaven —, *di omen avertant.*
forget, *obliviscor,*[3] *oblitus* (§ **50,** 4. *a*).
forgetting, *oblitus* (gen.).
forgive, *ignosco,*[3] *novi.*
fork, *furca, ae.*
form (v.), *facio, capio.*[3]
form (n.), *forma, ae;* (political) *institutum, i.*
former (the), *ille, a, ud.*
forsaken, *desertus.*
forth: to go —, *egredi.*
fortify, *munio.*[4]
fortitude, *fortitudo, inis* (F.).
fortress, *castellum, i* (N.).
fortune, *fortuna.*
forum, *forum, i.*
forward: to come, *exsistere.*
found, *condo,*[3] *didi;* to — a colony at, *coloniam deducere* (with acc.).
franchise, *civitas, atis* (F.), *jus, juris* (N.).

free, *liber, era, um;* — (as a gift), *gratuitus;* — town, *municipium;* freedom, *libertas.*
friend, *amicus, i;* intimate —, *familiaris.*
friendly, to be, *faveo,*[2] *favi.*
friendship, *amicitia, ae.*
fringe, *praetexo,*[3] *ui.*
from (out of), *ex;* (away from), *ab;* (by reason of), *propter* (see p. 33).
frugal, *parcus.*
frugally, *frugaliter.*
fruit, *fructus, ūs.*
full, *plenus;* —measure, *summus.*
fully, *bene, plane.*
function, *munus, eris* (N.).
furious, *ferox, ocis.*
further (adj.), *reliquus.*
fury, *saevitia, ae, furor, oris* (M.).
future, *futurus.*

G.

Gabinian law, *Gabinia lex.*
gain (v.), *pario,*[3] *peperi, partum;* *sibi conciliare.*
gain (n.), *quaestus, ūs.*
gain over, *concilio.*[1]
gallant, *fortissimus.*
galley, *navis, is* (F.).
games, *ludi, orum.*
gap, *hiatus, ūs* (M.).
garment, *vestis, is* (F.).
gate, *janua, porta, ae* (F.).
gather, *carpo,*[3] *psi.*
Gaul (the land), *Gallia, ae;* (the people), *Galli, orum.*
gay, *laetus.*
general (n.), *imperator, oris.*

generally, *fere* (see "men"), *vulgo.*

genius (intellect), *ingenium, i.*

German, *Germanus.*

get, *adipiscor;* — away, *effugio.*

getting round, *circumfusi.*

gift, *donum, i; munus, eris.*

gifts, *bona, orum.*

gigantic, *ingens, tis, immanis, e.*

give, *do,*[1] *dedi, datum; tribuo,*[3] *adhibeo;*[2] — back, *reddo;*[3] — new strength; — place, *cedo,*[3] *cessi;* — to one's self,*sumo.*[3]

glory (v.), *glorior.*[1]

glory (n.), *gloria, ae, laus, dis* (F.), *decus, oris* (N.), *fama, ae.*

go, *eo, ire, ivi, itum; procedo,*[3] *iter facio;*[3] — on behind, *sequor;*[3] — out, *egredi,*[3] *excedo,*[3] *exire;* — up to, *adire, accedere;* so goes, *ita se habet.*

goat, *caper, pri* (M.).

god, *deus, i* (§ 10, 4. *f*).

good, *bonus;* make —, *compensare;* be — for, *convenire* (dat.).

goodness, *virtus, utis* (F.).

governor, *praefectus, i.*

grandson, *nepos, otis.*

gratitude, occasion of, *gratum, res grata.*

great, *magnus, immanis.*

greatly, *multum;* so —, *tantum, magnifice.*

Grecian, Greek, *Graecus.*

greeting, *salutatio, onis* (F.).

grief, *luctus, us* (M.); *dolor, oris,* (M.).

groan, *gemitus, us* (M.).

gross, *gravis, e.*

ground, *terra;* on the —, *humi.*

group, *agmen, inis* (N.).

grow up, *adolesco,*[3] *evi;* — out, *provenio.*[4]

guard (n.), *custos, odis.*

gust, *flatus, us* (M.).

H.

habitation, *domicilium, i.*

hail, *appello.*[1]

hall, *aula, ae.*

halt, *consisto.*[3]

hand, *manus, us* (F.); holding in —, *ipse manu tenens;* (power), *potestas, atis* (F.)

Hannibal, *Hannibal, alis.*

happen, *accido.*[3]

happiness, *felicitas, atis* (F.).

happy, *felix, icis.*

harbinger, *praenuntia, ae.*

harbor, *portus, us* (M.).

hardship, *labor, oris* (M.).

hardy, *durus.*

harsh treatment, *crudelitas, atis* (F.).

Hasdrubal, *Hasdrubal, alis.*

hasten, *propero.*[1]

hastily, *temere.*

hateful, *odiosus.*

hatred, *odium, i.*

haughty, *arrogans, tis.*

have, *habeo,*[2] *ui, itum;* (take to one's self), *adhibeo*[2] (see p. 84).

head (n.), *caput, itis* (N.).

head-quarters, *castra;* appointed to —, *praefectus,* with gen.

health (state of), *valetudo, inis* (F.).

hear, *audio.*[4]

heart, *animus, i.*
heat, *calor, oris* (M.).
heaven, *caelum, i.*
heifer, *juvenca, ae.*
heir, *heres, edis.*
help, *auxilium, i.*
herald, *fetialis, is.*
herdsman, *pastor, oris.*
here, *hic ;* — and there, *passim.*
hereditary, *paternus.*
heritage, *hereditas, atis* (F.).
Hesiod, *Hesiodus, i.*
high, *altus, excelsus.*
highest, *summus, maximus.*
hill, *mons, collis* (M.).
hinder, *impedio.*[4]
hindrance, *impedimentum, i* (N.).
his (of his), *ejus ;* reflexive, *suus.*
history, *historia, ae.*
hold, *teneo ;*[2] — out, *propono.*
holiday, *dies festus.*
home, *domus, ūs ; domicilium, i ;* at —, *domi.*
Homer, *Homerus, i.*
honest men, *boni, orum.*
honesty, *probitas, atis* (F.).
honey, *mel, mellis* (N.).
honor (v.), *colo,*[3] *ui, cultum.*
honor (n.), *decus, ŏris* (N.) ; *honor, oris* (M.) ; *dignitas, atis* (F.) ; with — , *honeste.*
honorable, *honorificus.*
hope (n.), *spes, spei* (F.) ; *votum, i.*
hopeless, *inutilis, e.*
Horace, *Horatius, i.*
Horatian, *Horatius.*
horn, *cornu, us* (N.).
horse, *equus, i ;* war-horse, *equus militaris.*

hostile (of the enemy), *hostilis, e ;* (actively hostile), *infensus.*
hostilities, *bellum.*
hour, *hora, ae ;* in an —, *momento temporis.*
house, *domus, ūs* (F.).
how, *quam ;* — much, *quantum, quanto ;* interrog., *quomodo.*
however, *tamen, vero, quamvis ;* — large, *quantum vis.*
human, *humanus.*
humble, *humilis, e.*
humbled, *fractus.*
humiliation, *molestia, ae.*
humility, with great, *humillime.*
hunger, *fames, is* (F.).
hunter, *venator, oris.*
hurry (v.), *propero.*[1]
hurtful, to be, *noceo,*[2] *ui.*
husband, *maritus, i.*

I.

I, *ego ;* I for my part, *ego vero* (or *equidem*).
ides, *idūs, uum* (§ 84).
idleness, *socordia, ae.* — if, *si.*
ignorance, *inscitia, ae.*
ignorant, *ignarus.*
ill, *male.*
illustrious, *clarus, praeclarus.*
Illyrians, *Illyrii, orum.*
image, *imago, inis* (F.).
imitate, *imitor.*[1]
imitation, *imitatio, onis* (F.).
immediately, *statim, illico.*
immortal, *sempiternus.*
immovable, *immobilis, e.*
impart, *communico*[1] *cum.*
impatient, *impatiens, tis.*

impend, *impendeo.*[2]
implore, *oro.*[1]
important, *potens, tis.*
impression, see **memory.**
improper, *minus aptus.*
in, *in, de* (abl.).
increase (v. a.), *adaugeo,*[2] *xi,*
ctum (in neut. sense, use passive).
increasing, *major, us.*
indeed, *quidem.*
independence, *libertas, atis* (F.).
indifference to, *contemptio,*
onis (F.) (with gen.).
indignation, *ira, ae, indignatio,*
onis (F.).
indolence, *ignavia, ae.*
induce, *induco.*[3]
infamous, *turpis, e, nefandus.*
infamy, *ignominia, ae.*
inferior, *inferior, us.*
infinite, *summus.*
inflict death on, *morte multare.*
influence, to have, *gratiā valeo.*[2]
influenced, *adfectus.*
inform, *certiorem facio.*
inhabit, *habito.*[1]
inherit, *accipio.*[3]
inheritance, *hereditas, atis* (F.).
injury, *injuria, ae ;* do no —,
nihil nocere (dat.).
insolently, *insolenter.*
inspiration, *spiritus, ūs* (M.).
inspire, *animum dare ;* may the
gods —, *di duint.*
instance, for, *quidem.*
instantly, *statim.*
instead of, *pro* (abl.); *in loco*
(with gen.).
instil, *instillo*[1] (acc. and dat.).
institute, *constituo,*[3] *instituo.*[3]

instructed, *certior factus.*
insult (n.), *contumelia, ae.*
insurgents, use *seditio.*
intelligence, *intelligentia, ae.*
intend, *in animo esse (habere).*
intention, *consilium, i.*
intercede, *deprecor.*[1]
interest, to be one's —, *inter*
esse (gen. § 50, 4. *d*).
interests, *utilitates et commoda.*
interregnum, *interregnum, i.*
interrupt, *interrumpo,*[3] *rupi.*
interval, *tempus, oris* (N.).
intimate (adj. or noun), *famili-*
aris, is.
into, *in* (acc.).
intolerable, *intolerabilis, e.*
introduce, *induco,*[3] *duxi.*
invade, *invado,*[3] *di, sum.*
invaders, *hostes inrumpentes.*
invasion, *inruptio, onis* (F.).
invent, *invenio.*[4]
invention, *inventa, orum* (N.).
inventor, *inventor, toris* (M.).
inventress, *inventrix, tricis*
(F.).
inviolable, *inviolatus.*
invite, *invito,*[1] *oro.*[1]
irritated, *moleste ferens.*
island, *insula, ae.*
Italian, *Italus.*
Italy, *Italia, ae.*
ivory, *ebur, ŏris* (N.) ; of ivory,
eburneus.
Insubrians, *Insubres, ium.*

J.

jealous, *invidus* (gen.).
jealousy, *invidia, ae.*
jest, *jocus, i ;* pl. *joca.*

join in, *accedere ad, jungere se*
(dat.) ; in a military sense,
militare cum aliquo.
joined to, *conjunctus cum.*
joy, *gaudium, i.*   [*tri.*
judge (n.), *judex, icis, arbiter,*
judicial power, *judicium, i.*
Jugurtha, *Jugurtha, ae ;* (adj.),
Jugurthinus.
Julian (adj.), *Julius, a, um.*
Jupiter, *Juppiter, Jovis.*
just, *justus.*
just now, *nunc maxime.*
justice, *aequitas, tatis; justitia,*
ae.

K.

keep, *servo;* [1] — silence, *taceo.* [2]
kill, *interficio,* [3] *occīdo.* [3]
kind, *comis, e, benevolus.*
kindle, *incendo.* [3]
kindly, *comiter, blande.*
kindness, *beneficium, i ;* as a
quality, *comitas, facilitas, atis*
(F.), *benevolentia, ae.*
king, *rex, regis ;* (adj.), *regius.*
kingdom, *regnum, i.*
knee, *genu, us* (M.).
knife, *cultellus, i.*
knight, *eques, itis.*
know, *scio,* [4] *nosco,* [3] *novi ; intel-*
lego ; [3] (be aware), *sentio.* [4]
knowledge, *scientia, ae.*

L.

labor, *labor, oris* (M).
lake, *lacus, ūs* (M.).
lament, *moleste ferre.*

lamp, *lucerna, ae.*
land, *terra, ae.*
language, *oratio, onis ; verba.*
large, *magnus.*
lasting, *diuturnus.*
last, *duro.* [1]
last (adj.), *ultimus ;* at —, *tan-*
dem, extremum.
lastly, *denique.*
latest, *supremus.*
lastly, *denique.*
Latium (of), *Latinus, a, um.*
latter (the), *hic, haec, hoc* (see
p. 13).
law, *lex, legis* (F.).
lay, *impono;* [3]— hand on, *tango.*
lay hold, *teneo,* [2] *tango.* [3]
lay down, *deponere.*
lead (v.), *duco,* [3] *adduco,* [3] *duxi,*
ductum ; — away, *abduco.* [3]
leader, *dux, ducis.*
leap into, *insilio,* [4] *ui ;* — over,
transilio, [4] *ui.*
learn, *disco,* [3] *didici.*
learned, *doctus.*—at least, *saltem.*
leathern, *ex pellibus factus.*
leave, *relinquo,* [3] *liqui ;* (go from),
egredi ; (proceed), *proficisci.*
left (hand), *sinistra, ae.*
legion, *legio, onis* (F.).
length, at, *tandem, nunc demum.*
less, *inferior, us ; minus.*
let fall, *demittere.*
let loose, *libero.* [1]
lethargy, *stupor, oris* (M.).
letter, *epistola (ula), ae.*
levy, *conscribo.* [3]
liar, *mendax, acis.*
libation, *libamentum, i.*
liberate, *libero.* [1]
liberator, *liberator, toris.*

liberty, *libertas, tatis* (F.).
liberties, *jura* (N.).
Libyan, *Libycus.*
lie, *jaceo,*² *ui ;* — upon, *esse* (gen.).
life, *vita, ae ;* in the life-time of,
lift, *tollo,*³ *sustuli.* [*vivus* (abl.).
light (adj.), *levis, e.*
lighted (illuminated), *inlustra-
tus ;* (kindled), *accensus.*
like (adj.), *similis, e* (gen. or
dat.) ; (adv.), *velut, ut.*
lineage, *genus, eris.*
linger, *moror.*¹
lion, *leo, onis* (M.).
listen (to), *audio.*⁴
literature, *litterae, arum.*
little, *paulum ;* how — (adv.),
quam non ; distance, *paulum.*
live (v.), *vivo,*³ *vixi ;* *habito.*¹
long, *longus, diuturnus ;* —
since, *jamdudum ;* as — as,
quamdiu ; no longer, *non jam.*
look out, *prospicio ;* like, *videor.*
loose (let), *libero,*¹ *emitto.*³
loquacious, *loquax, acis.*
lord, *dominus, i ;* to be —,
potior ⁴ (gen. § 54, 6. *d*).
lose, *amitto.*³
loss, *detrimentum, i.*
loudly, *vehementer.*
love (n.), *amor, oris* (M.); *cari-
tas, atis* (F.) ; lover, *amans.*
lower, *inferior, us.*
lust, *cupido, inis* (F.).
luxuriously, *luxuriose.*

M.

Macedonian, *Macedonicus ;* a
Macedonian, *Macedo, nis.*

mad scheme or conduct, *furor.*
magnitude, *magnitudo.*
magistrate, *magistratus, ūs.*
maintain, *defendo.*³
make, *facio,*⁸ *feci ;* *reddo ;* ³ —
good, *compenso ;*¹ — way,
cedo ; ³ — for (seek), *peto.*³
man, *homo, inis, vir, i* (M.) ;
men generally, *magna pars
hominum ;* a man who, *is qui.*
manner, *mos, moris* (M.).
many, *multi, plurimi ;* so —,
tot ; very —, *plerique.*
March, (of), *Martius.*
march (v.), *proficiscor,*⁰ *profec-
tus ;* *progredior,*³ *gressus ;* *iter
facere.* — margin, *ora.*
march (n.), *iter, itineris* (N.).
mariner, *nauta, ae* (M.).
market-place, *forum, i.*
marriage, *matrimonium, i ;* —
with, *conubium ;* to give in —,
nuptum dare.
marry (of the man), *duco,*³ *duxi*
(sc. *in matrimonium,* or *uxo-
rem* in appos.) ; of the woman,
*nubo,*³ *nupsi* (with dat.).
Mars, *Mars, Martis.*
Marsian, *Marsus.*
martial, *bellicus.*
marvellous, *mirus.*
mask, *persona, ae.*
mass (of troops), *caterva, ae.*
massacre (v.), *trucido.*¹
massacre (n.), *caedes, is ;* *truci-
datio civium.*
master, *dominus, i.*
matron, *matrona, ae.*
may, *licet* (impers.), *possum.*
mean-time, *interea ;* means, *opes.*
measure, *consilium, i* (M.).

mediation, *deprecatio, onis* (F.).

meet, *occurro,*[3] *nanciscor,*[3] *nactus, invenio.*[4]

memorable, *memorabilis, e.*

memory, *memoria, ae;* our memories excited by our impressions, *animis memoria plenis recenti earum rerum quas sensibus percepimus.*

men (soldiers), *milites, um.*

menial, *servus, i.*

mercy, *clementia, ae.*

merit, *virtus, utis* (F.).

message, *mandatum, i.*

midst of, *medius.*

mighty, *magnus ille.*

might, *possim* (subj.).

Milan, *Mediolanum, i.*

military, *bellicus, militaris, e.*

mind, *mens, tis; animus, i.*

mine, *cuniculi, orum.*

mingle, *misceor.*[2]

misery, *miseria, ae.*

misuse, *pravus usus.*

Mithridatic, *Mithridaticus.*

model, *exemplum, i.*

moderate, *modicus.*

modern, *hodiernus.*

monarchy, *imperium, i.*

money, *pecunia, ae.*

monstrous, *immanis, e.*

morass, *palus, udis* (F.).

more, *plus, amplius, magis.*

morning, in the —, *mane* (N.); (adj.), *matutinus.* [*dies.*

morrow (next day), *posterus*

mortal, *mortalis, e.*

most (men), *plerique;* (adv.), *maxime.*

mother, *mater, tris.*

motive, *causa, ae.*

mountain, *mons, tis* (M.); (adj.), *montanus.*

mountaineer, *montanus.*

mourning, *luctus, ūs* (M.).

mouth, *os, oris* (N.); of river, *ostium, i.*

move, *moveo,*[2] *movi.*

moved, *permotus.*

movement, *motus, ūs* (M.).

moving, *incedens, tis.*

much, *multum, multo, magni.*

multiply, *multiplico.*[1]

multitude, *multitudo, inis* (F.).

Mulvian, *Mulvius.*

municipal law, *jus civile.*

murder (v.), *occido,*[3] *trucido.*[1]

murder (n.), *caedes, is.*

mutter, *summissa voce dicere.*

my, *meus, a, um* (VOC. M. *mi*).

myself, *ego.*

mysterious, *secretus.*

monument, *monumentum.*

N.

name (appoint), *creo.*[1]

name, *nomen;* in the —, *verbis.*

narrow, *tenuis, e; angustus, a, um;* narrow pass, *angustiae.*

nation, *gens, tis; natio, onis.*

nature, *natura, ae.*

naval, *navalis, e.*

near, *vicinus;* (prep.), *prope;* (adv.), *juxta, haud procul;* nearest relatives, *proximi.*

nearly, *paene.* [I. *d*).

necessary, *opus* (in pred. § 54,

need, *requiro;*[3] to have —, *opus esse* (dat. and abl.) ; to be in —, *egere.*

Vocabulary.

neglect, *neglego.*[3]

negligence (act of), *delictum, i.*

neighbor, *vicinus, finitimus, a, um.*

neighborhood, *vicinia, ae, vicinum, i.*

negligence, *negligentia, ae.*

nest, *nidus, i* (M.).

never, *nunquam.*

nevertheless, *nihilo minus.*

new, *novus.*

next (of two), *posterus;* of several, *proximus.* [*noctu.*

night, *nox, noctis* (F.) ; at —,

no (adj.), *nullus;* (adv.), *nihil.*

nobility, *nobilitas, atis* (F.).

noble, *nobilis, e* (to emphasize quality, use superlative) ; nobles (as a party), *nobilitas.*

noblest, *summus.*

not, *non;* as question, *nonne;* — to, *ne;* if —, *si minus.*

nothing, *nihil, nec quicquam.*

now, *nunc;* (already), *jam;* (of past time), *tum;* (emph.), *hic nunc;* (at this age), *hoc aetatis.*

number, *numerus, i;* great numbers, *multitudo.*

numerous, *magnus.*

Numidian, *Numida, ae.*

O.

oath, *jusjurandum* (§ 14, 2. *d*).

obedience, *obedientia;* unconditional —, *obed. omnium rerum.*

obey, *pareo,*[2] *ui, itum.*

object, *causa, ae;* (definite) *consilium, i.*

obliged, *coactus* (part. of *cogo*).

observe, *animadverto.*[3]

obstacle, *difficultas.*

obtain, *adsequor, consequor,*[3] *secutus; adipiscor,*[3] *adeptus.*

occasion, *occasio, tempus.*

occur, *fio, fieri, factus.*

ocean, *oceanus, i* (M.).

odious, *invisus.*

of, usually expressed by gen. or possessive (see p. 35).

offensive, *odiosus.*

offer (v.), *offerre, polliceri, praestare, imponere.*

offer (n.), *condicio, onis* (F.).

office, *magistratus, ūs; dignitas.*

officer, *praefectus, i.*

often, *saepe.*

oil, *oleum, i.*

old, *vetus, eris;* (of age), *natus.*

old age, *senectus, tutis* (F.).

old man, *senex, senis.*

older, *major.*

omen, *omen, inis* (N.).

on, *in* (abl.); —, *de.* [*sus.*

once, *quondam;* — more, *rursus,* *unus* (gen. *ius*); the — . . . the other, *alter* . . . *alter.* — at once, *statim.*

only (adj.), *solus* (gen. *ius*), *unicus;* (adv.), *modo, solum, tantum.*

onset, *impetus, ūs* (M.).

open (v.), *recludo,*[3] *si, sum.*

opinion, *sententia, ae.*

opportunity (favorable), *occasio, onis.*

oppose, *resisto,*[3] *stiti.*

opposed, *contrarius;* — in war, *adversus aliquem pugnare.*

opposite, *contra, alter, a, um.*

opposition, *oppositio, onis.*
oppression in one's province, *repetundae.*
oppressive, *gravis, e.*
or, *aut, vel;* (as altern.) *an, - ne* (§ **71**, 2).
oracle, *oraculum, i.*
oration, *oratio, onis* (F.).
orator, *orator, oris;* (adj.), *oratorius.*
order (v.), *jubeo,*[2] *jussi.*
order, *mandatum, i;* by — of, *jussu;* (rank), *ordo, inis.*
other, *alius, a, ud;* (of two), *aliter* (§ **47**, 9), *ceteri, reliqui;* some —, *aliquis.*
ought, *debeo,*[2] *oportet* (impers. with acc.).
our, *noster, tra, trum.*
out, *ex* (in compos.).
outlive (to have), *superstes esse.*
outside (prep.), *extra.*
over, *supra, trans* (acc.)
overcome, *supero.*[1]
overflowed, *superfusus.*
overhear, *excipio.*[3]
overflow, *se effundere per* (acc.).
overturn (neut.), *evertor.*[3]
overwhelmed, *confectus.*
owe, *debeo,*[2] *ui.*
own (often omitted), gen. of *ipse* in appos. with possessive ; *proprius.*

P.

painstaking, *diligentia, ae.*
Palatine, *Palatinus, i.*
palm-tree, *palma, ae.*

Pamphylia, *Pamphylia, ae;* (adj.), *Pamphyliensis.*
pang, *dolor, oris* (M.).
pardon (v.), *ignosco, novi.*
pardon (n.), *venia, ae.*
parent, *parens, tis.*
part, *pars, tis* (F.), (meaning duty, &c., use plur.) ; for the most —, *magna ex parte.*
partisan, *fautor, oris.*
partly, *aliqua (magna) ex parte.*
party, *pars, tis* (F.) (generally plur.) ; *factio, onis.*
pass a law, *legem ferre;* — over, *supero,*[1] *praetergredi, praeterferri*; (time), *ago.*[3]
passion (for), *cupiditas, atis* (F.) (gen.) ; passions, *perturbationes animi.*
patience, *patientia, ae.*
patrician, *patricius.*
patron, *patronus, i.*
pay, *solvo.*[3]
peace, *pax, pacis;* in —, *concors, dis.*
peaceful, *quietus.*
peculiar, *proprius.*
Penates, *Penates, ium* (M.).
penetrate, *penetro.*[1]
peninsula, *peninsula, ae.*
people, *populus, i* (M.), *plebs, is* (F.), *homines.*
perfection, in, *perfecte.*
perform, *ago,*[3] *fungor.*[3]
peril, *periculum, i.*
perish, *pereo, ire, ii.*
perpetual, *sempiternus.*
Perses, *Perses, is.*
persuade, *persuadeo*[2] (dat) ; friendly persuasion, *amica verba.*

Pharsalus, *Pharsalus, i;* (adj.),
  Pharsalicus.
Philip, *Philippus, i.*
Philometor, *Philometor, ŏris,*
  acc. *ora.*
philosopher, *philosophus, i.*
Physcon, *Physcon, onis.*
pilgrim, *peregrinator, oris.*
pillar, *columna, ae.*
pipe, *tibia, ae.*
pirate, *praedo, onis.*
pity (v.), have — on, *misereor* [2]
  (gen. person).
place (v.), *impono,*[3] *depono;* [3] —
  at the head, *praepono* [3] (dat.).
place (n.), *locus, i;* pl. *loca,*
  orum.
play (on instrument), *cano;* [3] —
  a part, *partes agere.*
player, *histrio, onis.*
pleasant, *commodus.*
please, *placeo,*[2] *ui, itum;* (wish),
  volo.
pleasure, *voluptas, atis* (F.).
pleasure-grounds, *horti deli-*
  cati.
plebeian, *plebeius.*
pledge, *polliceor.*[2]
plot, *conjuratio, onis* (F.).
plunder, *praeda, ae.*
plunge, *inicio,*[3] *jeci.*
poet, *poeta, ae* (M.).
poetry. *versus, uum* (pl.) (M.).
point out, *indico.*[1]
poison, *venenum, i.*
polished, *excultus.*
pollution, *violare.*
Pompey, *Pompeius, i;* (adj.),
  -anus.
poor, *miser, era, um; pauper,*
  eris.

populace, *vulgus, i* (N.).
population, *multitudo homi-*
  num.
position, *locus, i* (pl. *loca*).
possession, *possessio, onis, ager,*
  gri. — posterity, *posteri* (pl.).
posted, *collocatus.*
pour (neut.), *se fundere.*
poverty, *egestas, atis* (F.)
power, *potestas, atis* (F.); (dominion), *imperium, i* (N.);
  potentia, ae (F.).
powerful, *potens, tis.*
praise (v.), *laudo.*[1]
praise (n.), *laus, dis* (F.).
pray, *precor.*[1]
prayer, *carmen precationis.*
precede, *anteeo, ire.*
prediction, *vaticinatio, onis* (F.).
preparations, to make military
  —, *copias parare.*
prepare (a way), *munio.*[4]
prepared, *paratus.*
present (n.), *munus, eris* (N.).
present (adj.), *praesens, tis.*
preserve, *conservo.*[1]
preserver, *conservator, oris.*
prevail, *vinco.*[3]
prevent, *impedio.*[4]
priest, *sacerdos, otis, pontifex,*
  icis.
principal, *maximus.*
prison, *carcer, eris* (M.).
prisoner, *captivus, i.*
private (citizen), *privatus, i.*
privation, *inopia omnium re-*
  rum.
prize, *praemium, i.*
proceed, *progredior.*[3]
produce, *efficio.*[3]
professed, *apertus.*

professions (verbal), *verba, pro-missa.*
profit (v.), *fructum capere.*
profligacy, *flagitia, orum.*
promise (v.), *promitto,*[3] *polli-ceor,*[2] *itus ; edico.*[3]
promise (n.), *promissum, i.*
promontory, *promuntorium, i.*
proof, *testimonium, i.*
property, *bona, orum.*
propose, *fero, ferre.*
proscribe, *proscribo.*[3]
proscription, *proscriptio, onis* [(F.).
prosecute, *persequor.*[3]
prospect (in), *ante oculos.*
prostrate, *prostratus.*
proud, *superbus.*
proudly, *superbe.*
prove (try), *experior.*[4]
province, *provincia, ae.*
provision, to make, *provideo.*[2]
provisions, *commeatus, uum.*
public, *publicus.*
Punic, *Punicus.*
purchase, *emo,*[3] *emi, emptum.*
pure, *purus.*
purple, *purpureus.* [—, *qua re.*
purpose, *consilium, i ;* for what
pursue, *persequor ;*[3] *celeriter ad consectandum,* in hot pursuit.
push (against), *trudo.*[3]
put, *pono,*[3] *posui, positum ; —* an end to, *finio ;*[4] — to death, *interficio ;*[3] — off (shore), *sol-vere navem.*

Q.

quaestor, *quaestor, oris.*
quality (good), *virtus, utis* (F.).

quarter (district), *vicus, i* (M.).
quickly, *celeriter.*
quiet, *quies, etis* (F.).
quiet, *quietus ;* remain —, *qui-esco,*[3] *evi.*
quietly, *quiete.*
quit, *relinquo,*[3] *reliqui.*
quite, *admodum.*
quoth, *inquit* (after the first word or words of the quota-tion).

R.

rage, *ira.*
raging, *iratus, furens, tis.*
rags, *squalor, oris* (M.).
raise, *tollo,*[3] *sustuli, sublatum.*
rank, *ordo, inis* (M.).
rascal, *improbus, i.*
rather, *potius.*
reach, *manus, uum* (F.).
read (aloud), *recito.*[1]
reader, *lector, oris.*
ready, *paratus ad.*
real, *verus.*
reap (fruit), *capere.*
reason, *ratio, onis* (F.), *res, rei* (F.).
reawaken, *denuo concito.*[1]
recall, *revoco.*[1]
receive, *accipio*[3] (*excipio*), *cepi, ceptum.*
recognize, *agnosco,*[3] *novi ;* (hold valid), *ratum habere.*
recollection, *recordatio.*
recommend, *commendo.*[1]
recommendation, *commenda-tio, onis* (F.).
recompense, to make, *compen-sare.*
recount, *memoro, commemoro.*[1]

Vocabulary.

109

recourse, to have, *se conferre ad.*
recover, *recupero.*[1]
recovering, *experrectus.*
redeem, *compenso.*[1]
reed, *arundo, inis* (F.)
reedy, *arundinibus praetextus.*
refinement, *humanitas, atis* (F.).
refuge, *perfugium, i;* take —, *confugio.*[3]
refusal, *recusatio, onis.*
refuse, *recuso.*[1]
regain, *recipio.*[3]
regard (think), *existimo;*[1] — for, *studium* (gen.) ; pay —, *rationem habere, respicere;* re-gret, *dolor, oris.* [garding, *de.*
reign (v.), *regno.*[1]
reign (n.), *regnum, i.*
reject, *recuso,*[1] *eicio,*[3] *jeci.*
relation, to bear, *attineo.*[2]
relative, *propinquus.*
relief, *opis* (gen.), *em* (F.).
rely on, *confido*[3] (dat.).
relying, *fretus* (abl.).
remain, *maneo,*[2] *mansi.*
remainder of, remaining, *reliquus.*
remark, *animadverto.*[3]
remarkable, *insignis, e.*
remember, *recordor*[1] (§ 50, 4. *a,* R.).
remembrance, *recordatio, onis.*
remind, *moneo,*[2] *ui, itum.*
remnant, *reliquiae, arum.*
remote, *ultimus.*
remove, *averto,*[3] *amoveo.*[2]
renounce (allegiance to), *imperium abicere.*
renovate, *renovo.*[1]
renown, *laus, dis* (F.).

repay (a kindness), *referre.*
repent, *paenitet.*
repeat, *iterum* with verb.
reply, *respondeo,*[?] *di, sum.*
reply, *responsum, i.*
report, *nuntio,*[1] *dico.*[3]
represented, *expressus.*
representative, *exemplum, i.*
reprisals, to make, *compensare.*
republic, *respublica* (§ 14, 2. *d.*).
reputation, *fama, ae.*
require, *postulo.*[1]
rescue, *servo.*[1]
resentment, *simultas, atis* (F.), *iracundia, ae.*
reserve, *reservo;*[1] — to one's own use, *sibi adservare.*
residence, *domicilium, i.*
resign (office), *abdico;*[1] (power), *depono.*[3]
resist, *resisto,*[3] *stiti.* [ger.].
resistance, *contendere* (inf. or
resolution, *consilium, i.*
resolve, *constituo.*[3]
rest-of, *reliquus.*
restless, *inquietus.*
restore, *renovo,*[1] *restituo,*[3] *reddo.*[3]
retire, *abeo, ire* (abl.).
return, *revertor,*[3] *regredior,*[3] *redeo, respondeo;* on his —, *rediens, tis;* — thanks, *agere.*
return (n.), *reditus, ūs* (M.).
revenge, *ultio, onis* (F.).
revive (neuter), *renascor;*[3] (trans.), *restituo.*[3]
revolution, *civilis motus* (M.).
reward, *praemium, i;* to give as —, *donare.*
rich, *dives, itis, opimus.*
riches, *divitiae, arum.*

right, *rectus, a, um;* rights, *jura, um* (N.); to think —, *recte sentire.*

right hand, *dextra, ae.*

ring (signet-ring), *anulus, i.*

rise, *orior*[3] (infin. *oriri*), *coörior, ortus; surgo,*[3] *surrexi.*

rival, *aemulus, i.*

river, *flumen, inis* (N.).

road, *iter, itineris* (N.).

rob, *spolio.*[1]

robe, *toga, ae, vestis, is* (F.).

roll (for writing), *tabellae, arum.*

Roman, *Romanus.*

Rome, *Roma, ae;* (as people), *Romani;* (as state), *civitas Romana* (*respublica*).

room, *cubiculum, i.* [*radicitus.*

root, *radix, icis; —* and branch,

rose, *rosa, ae;* full of roses, *roseus. —* round, *circum.*

roving, *vagus.*

royal, of royalty, *regius.*

ruin, *exitium, i.*

rule over, *impero.*[1]

ruler, *princeps, ipis.*

rumor, *rumor, oris* (M.).

run, *curro,*[3] *cucurri.*

rush, *procurro;*[3] *—* upon, *inruo.*[3]

S.

Sabine, *Sabinus.*

sacred, *sacer, cra, um.*

sacrifice, *macto.*[1]

safe, *tutus.*

safety, *salus, utis* (F.).

sail (v.), *navigo.*[1]

sail (n.), *velum;* sailor, *nauta.*

sake: for the — of, *causā,* following a gen.

sallies of wit, *facetiae, arum.*

same, *idem, eadem, idem.*

sanctuary, *aedes, is.*

satellite, *satelles, itis.*

satisfied, *contentus.*

savage, *barbarus.*

save, *servo.*[1]

say, *dico,*[3] *aio, inquam* (Gr. p. 81); intr. *loquor.*

scarcely, *vix.—*scanty, *exiguus.*

schooled, *adsuefactus.*

scorn, *ludibrium.*

sea, *mare, is* (N.); (adj.), *marinus.*

sea-shore, *ora, ae.*

season, *tempus, oris* (N.).

seat, *sedes, is* (F.).

seated, *sedens, tis.*

secession, *secessio, onis* (F.).

second, *secundus, alter.*

second time, *iterum.*

secret, *res occulta; —* society, *sodalitas, atis* (F.).

secretary, *scriba, ae* (M.).

secure (v.), *occupo.*[1]

secure: to be —, *non dubiam spem habere;* to make —, *tutiorem reddere.*

security, *securitas, atis* (F.)

sedition, *seditio, onis* (F.).

see, *video,*[2] *vidi, visum.*

seek, *peto,*[3] *cupio,*[3] *adpeto.*[3]

seem, *videor,*[2] *visus.*

self-same, *idem, eadem, idem.*

seize, *prehendo,*[3] *di, sum; eripio.*[3]

sell, *vendo,*[3] *didi.*

senate, *senatus, ūs* (M.); — house, *curia, ae.*

senator, *senator, oris;* adj. *-ius.*

send, *mitto*,[3] *misi, missum.*
sense, *sensus, ūs* (M.).
sensible, *prudens, tis.*
sentence, to pass, *judicium ferre.*
separate, *separo.*[1]
separate (his own), *proprius.*
sepulchre, *sepulcrum, i.*
serious, *gravis, e.*
seriously, *in serium.*
Seriphus, *Seriphus, i* (F.); (adj.), *Seriphius.*
servant, *servus, i.*
serve, *servio;*[4] — well or ill, *bene aut male mereri de.*
servile, *servilis, e.*
session, *consessus, ūs* (but may be omitted; as, *in Senatum venire*).
set, *pono;*[3] — on foot, *incipio,*[3] *cepi, ceptum;* — out, *proficiscor,*[3] *fectus;* — sail, *navigo.*[1]
several, *plures, ium; singuli.*
severe, *severus.*
severely, *saeviter.*
severity, *severitas, atis* (F.).
shade, *umbra, ae.*
shaft, *telum, i* (N.).
shame, *ignominia, ae, dedecus, oris* (N.).
share (v.), *participo.*[1]
share (n.), *pars, tis* (F.).
she, *ea, illa.*
she-wolf, *lupa, ae.*
shelter, *tego,*[3] *texi, tectum.*
shepherd, *pastor, oris.*
ship, *navis, is* (F.).
shivered, *pulsus.*
shore, *litus, oris* (N.); go on —, *in terram egredi.*
short, *brevis, e.*

shortly after, *paulo post.*
should, &c., see p. 63.
show, *demonstro.*[1]
shrink, *abhorreo.*[2]
sick, to be, *aegroto.*[1]
sickness (sea-sickness), *nausea, ae.*
side (party), *pars, tis* (F.); on the —, *a parte.*
siege, for the siege of, *ad oppugnandum.*
sight, *conspectus, ūs* (M.), *spectaculum, i.*
sign, signal, *signum, i.*
signify, *significo.*[1]
silence, *silentium, i;* in —, *silentio, tacite;* to keep —, *silere, tacere.* [*modo.*
simple, *inconditus;* simply,
since, *post* (acc.; see p. 40); ever —, *jam inde; postea.*
singular, *mirus.*
sister, *soror, oris.*
sit, *sedeo,*[2] *sedi.* — situation, *res.*
skilful, *peritus* (gen.).
skill, *ars, artis* (F.).
slaughter, *caedes, is* (F.).
slave, *servus, i;* to be a —, *servio;*[4] — market, *grex venalium.*
slay, *interficio,*[3] *feci, fectum, caedo,*[3] *cecidi, caesus;* — with cruelty, *trucido.*[1]
slayer, *interfector, oris.*
slight, *parvus.*
sloth, *ignavia, ae.*
small, *parvus.*
smite, *percutio,*[3] *cussi.*
snake, *anguis, is, serpens, tis* (N.).
snatch, *eripio,*[3] *ui.*

so, *sic, ita ;* — .. as, *ita* . . *ut,*
tam . . *quam ;* — many, *tot ;*
— great, *tantus ;* — that, *adeo*
ut ; will have it so, *sic velle.*
soldier, *miles, itis.*
solicitous, *sollicitus.*
solid, *firmus.*
some, *aliquid, nonnullus* (p. 18);
— thing, *aliquid ;* — time,
aliquamdiu ; — times, *inter-*
dum ; —... others, *alii...alii.*
son, *filius, i ;* — -in-law, *gener,*
eri.
song, *carmen, inis* (N.).
soon, *brevi tempore ;* (present-
ly), *mox ;* — after, *paulo*
post ; as — as, *ut primum.*
soothsayer, *haruspex, icis.*
sorrow, *dolor, oris* (M.).
soul, *animus, i ; anima, ae.*
sound, *sanus.*[1]
south, *meridionalis, e.*
Spain, *Hispania, ae ;* (adj.),
Hispanicus.
spare, *parco,*[3] *peperci ;* (refrain),
tempero.[1] **Spartan.** *Spartanus.*
speak, *loquor,*[3] *locutus ;* — of,
commemoro.[1]
spectacle, *spectaculum, i.*
spectre, *species, ei* (F.).
speculator, *fenerator, oris.*
speech, *sermo, onis* (M.).
spirit, *animus, i* (M.), (pl.).
sport, *lusio, onis* (F.).
spot, *locus, i ;* plur., *loca.*
spring, *ver, veris* (N.).
square (of a city), *platea, ae.*
staff, *baculum, i.*
stand, *sto,*[8] *steti, statum ;* —
aside, *de via decedere ;* —
(bear), *ferre ;* (be), *esse.*

state, *civitas, atis ; res publica*
(F.).
stately, *procerus.*
statue, *statua, ae.*
stature, *statura, ae.*
steep, *arduus.*
steer, *guberno.*[1]
step aside, *decedo.*[8]
stepmother, *noverca, ae.*
stick (n.), *fustis, is* (M.).
stifle, *exstinguo.*[3]
still, *etiam tum, etiam nunc,*
adhuc.
stir up, *excito.*[1]
stone, *saxum, i.*
stop, *moror.*[1]
storm, violent, *magna tempes-*
tas.
story, *fabula, ae.*
straggle, *vagor.*[1]
stranded, *in terram delatus.*
strange, *novus.*
stream, *flumen, inis* (N.).
strength, *vires, ium* (F.).
strengthen, *confirmo.*[1]
stretching, *patens, tis.*
strict, *severus, exactus.*
strictly, *severe.*
strike, *percutio ;*[3] — down, *cae-*
do ;[3] — a blow, *inferre.*
striking (keen), *argutus.*
stroke, *mulceo,*[2] *mulsi.*
strong, *validus.*
stronghold, *praesidium, i.*
strongly, *vehementer.*
studious, *studiosus.*
stupidity, *stultitia, ae.*
subject, to be, *servire.*
subjects, *cives, ium.*
submission, *obsequium, i.*
submit, *se dedere.*

subterranean, *subterraneus.*
succeed, *succedo,*[3] *cessi.*
success, *prosperus eventus, successus, ūs* (M.).
successful, *felix, icis.*
succor (help), *subvenire.*
suckle, *lacto.*[1]
such, *talis, e; is, ea, id.*
sudden, *subitus.* [*subito.*
suddenly (on a sudden), *repente,*
suffer, *fero, tuli; patior.*[3]
sufficiency, *satis.* [*consciscere.*
suicide, to commit, *mortem sibi*
suit, *convenio.*[4] ·
suitable, *idoneus.*
summer, *aestas, atis* (F.); (adj.), *aestivus.*
summit, *summus mons.*
summon, *convoco.*[1]
sun, *sol, solis* (M.).
superior, *superior, melior;* (abs.), *optimus.*
support, *confirmo.*[1]
suppose, *puto.*[1]
supreme, *supremus, summus.*
surely, *profecto.*
surface of earth, *omnis terra.*
surmount, surpass, *supero.*[1]
surrender (v.), *dedo,*[3] *dedidi.*
surrender (n.), *deditio, onis* (F.).
surrounded, *stipatus.*
survive, *superesse, superstes* (*itis*) *esse* with dat.
suspend, *suspendo,*[3] *di, sum.*
suspense, *cura, ae.*
swallow (n.), *hirundo, inis* (F.).
swamp, *palus, udis* (F.).
swear, *juro;*[1] — together, *conjuro.*[1]
sweet, *dulcis, e.*
sweetly, *jucunde.*

swim, *no, nato, trano.*[1]
symptom, *indicium, i.*
Syracuse, *Syracusae, arum* (F.).
Syracusan, *Syracusanus, a, um.*
Syrian, *Syrus, a, um.*

T.

take, *capio,*[3] *cepi, captum, porto,*[1] *duco;*[3] (enjoy), *fruor*[3]; — away, *adimo,*[3] *emi, emptum;* — in charge, *accipio;*[3] — part in, *communico;*[1] — claim for one's self, *sibi adrogare;* — prisoner, *capere;* — refuge, *confugere;* — up arms, *arma capere;* — by the hand, *manu arripere;* (follow), *sequi;* — seriously, *in serium vertere.*
task, *opus, eris* (N.).
talents, *ingenium, i* (use sing.).
tall, *procerus.*
taunt, *obicio,*[3] *exprobro.*[1]
teach, *doceo,*[2] *ui.*
teacher, *doctor, oris.*
tear away, *detraho,*[3] *xi, ctum.*
tear (n.), *lacrima, ae.*
tell, *nuntio,*[1] *narro,*[1] *dico.*[3]
temperance, *temperantia, ae, continentia, ae.*
tempest, *tempestas, atis* (F.).
temple, *templum, i, aedes, is* (F.).
terms, *condiciones, um* (F.).
terrify, *terreo,*[2] *ui, itum.*
testimony, *testimonium, i.*
than, *quam,* (or abl.).
thanks, *grates, gratiae, arum.*
that, *ut, quod* (see pp. 54, 75); — not, *ne;* but —, *quin.*

the, often expressed by *ille.*

theatre,*scaena, ae.* thence,*inde.*

then, *tum, inde, deinde, igitur.*

there, *ibi.* — their, *eorum, suus.*

therefore, *itaque, qua de causa.*

thing, *res, rei* (F.).

think, *puto,*[1] *reor,*[2] *ratus.*

this, *hic, iste;* often *qui.*

this day's, *hodiernus.*

thong, *lorum, i.*

though, *quamquam, etiam si.*

thoughtlessness, *temeritas, atis* (F.).

thought, *consilium, i.*

thousand, *mille* (§ **18,** I. *e*) ; one of a —, *unus de multis.*

threaten, *minor, minitor* [1] (dat. of person) ; *impendeo* [2] (dat.).

thronged, *refertus.*

through, *per, propter,* or by abl.

throw, *jacio,*[3] *jeci, jactum;* — off, *abicio,*[3] *jeci.*

thrown (down), *dejectus.*

thus, *ita.*

Tiber, the river, *Tiberis, is* (M.) ; the river-god, *Tiberinus, i.*

till, *donec.* — timidity, *formido.*

time, *tempus, oris* (N.) ; for some —, *aliquamdiu;* from — to —, *interdum;* from that — forth, *jam inde;* at the same —, *tamen.*

tired, *fessus;* to be —, *taedet* (§ **50,** 4. *c*). [dative.

to, *ad* (acc.); often sign of

to-day, *hodie, nunc.*

together, *una.*

toil, *labor, oris* (M.).

tomb, *sepulcrum, i.* [*crastinus.*

to-morrow, *cras;* of —, (adj.),

tongue, *lingua, ae.*

too, *nimis;* or express by comparative; (also), *quoque.*

tooth, *dens, tis* (M.) ; grip of —, *morsus, ūs* (M.).

torch, *fax, facis* (F.).

torment (n.), *tormentum, i; cruciatus, ūs.*

torture (n.), *tormentum, i.*

towards, *erga* (acc.), *ad, versus.*

town, *municipium, i; oppidum, i;* (village), *vicus, i* (M.).

trace, *duco.*[3]

traitor, *proditor, oris.*

tranquillity, *tranquillitas, atis* (F.).

transaction, *res, rei* (F.).

transgress, *minus obediens esse* (dat.).

travel, *iter facere.*

traveller, *viator, oris.*

traverse, *transire.*

treachery, *perfidia, ae.*

treason, *majestas, atis* (§ **50,** 4. *b*).

treasury, *aerarium, i.*

treat, *tracto;* [1] — as a son, *in filii loco habere.*

treatise, *liber, bri.*

treaty, *indutiae, arum.*

tree, *arbor.* — trial, *tormenta.*

tribe, *tribus, ūs; gens, tis* (F.).

tribune, *tribunus, i.*

trifling, *minimus.*

tripod, *cortina, ae.* [*dis* (F.).

triumph, *triumphus, i; laus,*

triumphal, *triumphalis, e.*

troops, *milites, um.*

trouble, *res adversae* (plur.).

troubled, to be, *laborare.*

Troy, *Troja, ae;* of —, *Trojanus, a, um.*

true, *verus, a, um;* *quidem.*
trust, *confido.*[3]
trumpet, *tuba, ae.*
truth, *veritas, atis* (F.).
turf, *caespites, um* (plur.).
turn, *verto,*[1] *ti, sum;* — away, *avertor;* [3] — out-of-doors, *foras eicio.*[3]
tusk, *dens, tis* (M.).
two, *duo;* where only —, *ambo.*
tyranny, *dominatio, onis* (F.).
tyrant, *tyrannus, i.*

U.

Ufentine, *Ufens, tis.*
unambitious, *minime ambitiosus.*
uncle, *avunculus, i.*
uncover, *detego.*[3]
undaunted, *invictus.*
under, *sub* (acc. or abl.).
understand, *recte aestimo,*[1] *teneo.*[2]
undertake, *adgredior.*[3]
undoubtedly, *sine dubio.*
unfeeling, *durus.*
ungrateful, *ingratus.*
unjust, *injustus.*
unimpeached, *integer incolumisque.*
unhappy, *miser, era, um.*
universal, *communis, e.*
unless, *nisi.* — until, *donec.*
unprincipled, *improbus.*
unprofitable, *inutilis, e.*
unrighteous, *iniquus.*
unworthy, *indignus.*
upbraid, *obicio,*[3] *jeci.*
upper classes, *nobiles.*

upon (as living —), *ex.*
upward, *sursum.*
urge, *suadeo* [2] (dat.).
use (v.), *utor,*[3] *usus.*
use (n.), *usus, ūs* (M.).
useless, *inutilis, e.*
utmost (adj.), *maximus.*

V.

vast, *ingens, tis.*
vainly, *frustra, nequicquam.*
Valerian, *Valerius, a, um.*
valor, *virtus, utis* (F.).
value, *pretium, i.*
Veians, *Veientes, ium.*
vein, *vena, ae.*
vengeance, *ulcisci;* of —, use gerund.
venture, *audeo,*[2] *ausus.*
very, *per,* in compos. (§ 17, 5. *d*); — same, *ipse, a, um; graviter;* often by superl.
vice, *vitium, i.* — vessel, *navis.*
victim, *hostia, victima, ae* (F.).
victor, victorious, *victor, oris* (M.); *victrix, icis* (F.).
victory, *victoria, ae.*
view, *cogitatio, onis* (F.); *sententia, ae;* to be with a —, *pertinere ad.*
vigorous, *acer, cris; nervosus.*
violence, *vis* (F.).
violent, *violentus.*
violently, *vehementer, vi.*
virtue, *virtus, utis* (F.).
voluntary, *voluntarius.*
vote, *sententia, ae.*
vow, *votum, i.*

W.

wages, *merces, edis* (F.).
wait, *maneo,*[2] *mansi;* — for, *exspecto.*[1]
wall (of house), *paries, etis* (M.); (of city), *murus, i* (M.).
wander, *vagor.*[1]
want to, *opus esse* (dat. of person and abl. of thing); to be in — of, *indigere* (gen. of thing).
war, *bellum, i* (N.).
war-horse, *equus militaris.*
warlike, *bellicosus.*
warrior, *vir fortis.*
warn, *moneo;*[2] warning, *monitus.*
wasted, *confectus.*
watch, *observo.*[1]
water, *aqua, ae.*
wave, *fluctus, ūs* (M.).
way, *via, ae;* a good —, *aliquantum.*
weaken, *debilito.*[2]
wealth, *copiae, arum.*
wealthy, *locuples, tis.*
wear, *gero,*[3] *gessi, gestum.*
well, *bene.*
what? *quid?* — sort? *qualis?*
whatever, *quod,* with indic.
when, *cum, ubi, ut* (p. 67).
whenever, *cum* (with indic.).
where, *ubi, quo, qua* (§ **41**, 2. *a.*). [*sive.*
whether, *utrum .. an, sive ..*
which, rel., *quod; qualis, e;* int, while, *cum.* [*quis, uter* (p. 17).
white, *albus.*
whither, *quo.*
who, *qui;* whoever, *quisquis, quicumque, siquis.*

who? (interrog.) *quis* (see p. 17).
whole, *totus* (gen. *ius*).
wholly, *plane, omnino.*
why, *cur, quam ob rem.*
wide, *latus;* (of measure), *in latitudinem.*
wicked, *sceleratus.*
wife, *uxor, oris.*
wild, *ferus, immanis, e;* — beast, *fera;* — fig, *caprificus.*
will, *volo, velle, volui.*
willing, *paratus.*
willingly, *volens, tis.*
win, *concilio,*[1] *pario;*[3] — triumph, *triumphum ago.*[3]
wind, *ventus, i.*
window, *fenestra, ae.*
winter (v.), *hiberno.*[1]
wisdom, *consilium, i.*
wish, *volo, cupio,*[3] *opto.*[1]
with, *cum;* with me, *mecum;* — himself, &c., *secum.*
within, *intra, inter;* of time, often expressed by abl. (see p. 40).
without, *sine;* — doing a thing (see p. 60).
wolf, *lupus, i* (M.); *lupa, ae* (F.).
woman, *mulier, is.*
wonder (n.), *miraculum, i.*
wont, to be, *soleo,*[2] *solitus.*
woodpecker, *picus, i.*
word, *verbum, i.*
work, *ministerium, i.*
world, *orbis terrarum; homines, um;* in the —, *omnino.*
worn out (by age), *aetate confectus.*
worship, *colo,*[3] *colui, cultum.*
worst, *pessimus.*

worthy, *dignus* (with abl.).
would, &c., see p. 63.
wound, *vulnus, eris* (N.).
wounded, *vulneratus.*
wretched, *miser, era, um.*
write, *scribo,*[3] *psi, ptum; —*
down, *conscribo.*[3]
wrong, *pravus.*

Y.

year, *annus, i.*
yesterday, *heri;* of —, *hester-*
nus. [*etiam.*
yet, *tamen;* not —, *nondum*
you (sing.), *tu;* (plur.), *vos.*

young, *juvenis, is;* — man,
adulescens, tis; juvenis, is;
— of birds, *pullus, i.*
younger, *minor, oris.*
your (of sing. subject), *tuus, a,*
um; vester, tra, um.
yourself, *ipse* (tu), *te.*
yourselves, *ipsi, vos.*
youth, *puer, eri; juventus, tu-*
tis (F.) ; young man, *adules-*
cens, tis.

Z.

Zama (adj.), *Zamensis, e.*
zeal, *alacritas, atis* (F.).

Boston, September, 1875.

GINN BROTHERS,

Publishers,

11 Tremont Place, ... BOSTON.

Terms: Cash in Thirty Days.   **Wholesale and Retail Prices.**

ENGLISH.

Wholesale. Retail.

ARNOLD'S MANUAL of ENGLISH LITERATURE.
Historical and Critical. By THOMAS ARNOLD, M. A. $3.00

CARPENTER'S INTRODUCTION TO ANGLO-SAXON. An Introduction to the study of the Anglo-Saxon Language, Comprising an Elementary Grammar, Selections for Reading with Notes, and a Vocabulary. By STEPHEN H. CARPENTER, Professor of Logic and English Literature in the University of Wisconsin, and Author of "English of the XIV. Century." pp. 212 . . . . 1.00   1 25

CRAIK'S ENGLISH OF SHAKESPEARE. Illustrated in a Philological Commentary on his Julius Cæsar. by GEORGE L. CRAIK, Queen's College, Belfast. Edited by W. J. ROLFE, Cambridge. Cloth . . . 1.40   1.75

ELEMENTS OF THE ENGLISH LANGUAGE. An Introduction to the study of Grammar and Composition. By BERNARD BIGSBY. Univ. Oxon., Superintendent of Public Schools, Port Huron; Author of "The History of the English Language" 40   .50

ENGLISH OF THE XIV. CENTURY. Illustrated by Notes, Grammatical and Etymological, on Chaucer's Prologue and Knight's Tale. Designed to serve as an Introduction to the Critical Study of English. By STEPHEN H. CARPENTER, A. M., Professor of Rhetoric and English Literature in the State University of Wisconsin 1.40   1.75

HUDSON'S FAMILY SHAKESPEARE: Plays selected and prepared, with Notes and Introductions, for Use in Families.

Volume I., containing As You Like It, The Merchant of Venice, Twelfth Night, First and Second of King Henry the Fourth, Julius Cæsar, and Hamlet.
Volume II., containing The Tempest, The Winter's Tale, King Henry the Fifth, King Richard the Third, King Lear, Macbeth, and Antony and Cleopatra.
Volume III., containing A Midsummer Night's Dream, Much Ado about Nothing, King Henry the Eighth, Romeo and Juliet, Cymbeline, Coriolanus, and Othello.
And Hudson's Life, Art, and Characters of Shakespeare. 2 vols.

5 vols.   Cloth 8.00   10.00
        Half morocco 12.00   15.00
        Full calf 16.00   20.00

HUDSON'S LIFE, ART, AND CHARACTERS OF SHAKESPEARE. Including an Historical Sketch of the Origin and Growth of the Drama in England, with Studies in the Poet's Dramatic Architecture, Delineation of Character, Humor, Style, and Moral Spirit, also with Critical Discourses on the following plays, — A Midsummer Night's Dream, The Merchant of Venice, The Merry Wives of Windsor, Much Ado about Nothing, As You Like It, Twelfth Night, All's Well that Ends Well, Measure for Measure, The Tempest, The Winter's Tale, King John, King Richard the Second, King Henry the Fourth, King Henry the Fifth, King Richard the Third, King Henry the Eighth, Romeo and Juliet, Julius Cæsar, Hamlet, Macbeth, King Lear, Antony and Cleopatra, Othello, Cymbeline, and Coriolanus. In Two Volumes. Cloth 3.20   4.00

HUDSON'S SERMONS. 1.40   1.75

HUDSON'S SCHOOL SHAKESPEARE. 1st Series. $1.60 $2.00

Containing AS YOU LIKE IT,   THE TWO PARTS OF HENRY IV.,
THE MERCHANT OF VENICE,   JULIUS CÆSAR,
TWELFTH NIGHT,   HAMLET.
Selected and prepared for Use in Schools, Clubs, Classes, and Families. With Introductions and Notes. By the REV. HENRY N. HUDSON.

HUDSON'S SCHOOL SHAKESPEARE. 2d Series. 1.60 2.00

Containing THE TEMPEST,   KING RICHARD THE THIRD,
THE WINTER'S TALE,   KING LEAR,
KING HENRY THE FIFTH,   MACBETH, ANTONY AND CLEOPATRA.

HUDSON'S SCHOOL SHAKESPEARE. 3d Series. 1.60 2.00

. Containing A MIDSUMMER NIGHT'S DREAM,   ROMEO AND JULIET,
MUCH ADO ABOUT NOTHING,   CYMBELINE,
KING HENRY VIII.,   CORIOLANUS,
OTHELLO.

HUDSON'S SEPARATE PLAYS OF SHAKESPEARE.

THE MERCHANT OF VENICE. In Paper Cover	.32	.40
JULIUS CÆSAR. In Paper Cover	.32	.40
HAMLET. In Paper Cover	.32	.40
THE TEMPEST. In Paper Cover	.32	.40
MACBETH. In Paper Cover	.32	.40
HENRY THE EIGHTH. In Paper Cover	.32	.40
AS YOU LIKE IT	.32	.40
HENRY THE FOURTH. Part I.	.32	.40
KING LEAR.	32	.40
MUCH ADO ABOUT NOTHING	.32	.40
ROMEO AND JULIET	.32	.40
OTHELLO.	.32	.40

HALSEY'S GENEALOGICAL AND CHRONOLOGI-

CAL CHART of the Rulers of England, Scotland, France, Germany, and Spain. By C. S. HALSEY. Mounted, 33 × 48 inches. Folded and Bound in 4to, 10 × 12 inches 1.50

HALSEY'S BIBLE CHART OF GENEALOGY AND

CHRONOLOGY, from the Creation to A. D. 100. Prepared by C. S. HALSEY 1.00 1.25
This Chart is designed to illustrate Bible History by showing on a clear and simple plan the genealogy and chronology of the principal persons mentioned in the Scriptures.

HARVARD EXAMINATION PAPERS. Collected and

arranged by R. F. LEIGHTON, A. M., Master of Melrose High School. Second Edition, containing papers of June and September, 1874 . . . 1.25 1.56
These are all the questions (except on the subject of Geometry), in the form of papers, which have been used in the examinations for admission to Harvard College since 1860. They will furnish an excellent series of Questions in Modern, Physical, and Ancient Geography ; Grecian and Roman History ; Arithmetic and Algebra ; Plane and Solid Geometry ; Logarithms and Trigonometry ; Latin and Greek Grammar and Composition ; Physics and Mechanics. They have been published in this form for the convenience of Teachers, classes in High Schools, and especially for pupils preparing for college.

THE LIVING WORD; or, Bible Truths and Lessons .80 1.00

The distinguishing feature of this book is the arrangement by subjects of the spiritual and moral truths of the Bible, so that all its most expressive utterances upon a given subject may be read in unbroken succession. It is believed that this will furnish what has been long needed for public and private reading in the home, the school, and the church.

OUR WORLD, No. I.; or, First Lessons in Geography.

Revised edition, with new Maps, by MARY L. HALL . . . . .75 .94
Designed to give children clear and lasting impressions of the different countries and inhabitants of the earth rather than to tax the memory with mere names and details.

OUR WORLD, No. II.; or, Second Series of Lessons

in Geography. By MARY L. HALL. With fine illustrations of the various countries, the inhabitants and their occupations, and two distinct series of Maps, 5 pages physical, and 19 pages of finely engraved copperplates political $1.60 $2.00

This book is intended, if used in connection with the First Lessons, to cover the usual course of geographical study It is based upon the principle that it is more useful to give vivid conceptions of the physical features and political associations of different regions than to make pupils familiar with long lists of places and a great array of statistics.

PEIRCES TABLES OF LOGARITHMIC and TRIG-

ONOMETRIC FUNCTIONS TO THREE AND FOUR PLACES OF DECIMALS. By JAMES MILLS PEIRCE, University Professor of Mathematics at Harvard University. Cloth 60   .75

PEIRCE'S ELEMENTS OF LOGARITHMS; with an

Explanation of the Author's THREE AND FOUR PLACE TABLES. By JAMES MILLS PEIRCE, University Professor of Mathematics at Harvard University .80   1 00

This Work is a Companion to THREE AND FOUR PLACE TABLES OF LOGARITHMIC AND TRIGONOMETRIC FUNCTIONS, by the same Author.

REPRESENTATIVE AUTHORS. By H. H. MORGAN.

This is essentially a repertorium, and can be made equally useful as a work of reference and as a companion to any manual of literature, or as a guide in any course of reading. It presents the representative authors of England and America, — their mode of presenting their subjects, the literary forms which they employ, their representative works, their characterization by critics of established reputation The classification is at once simple and exhaustive, and meets a want not hitherto provided for.

STEWART'S ELEMENTARY PHYSICS. American

Edition. With QUESTIONS and EXERCISES. By PROF. G. A. HILL, of Harvard University 1.40   1.75

The Questions will be direct and exhaustive upon the text of Mr. Stewart's work. After the Questions will be given a series of easy Exercises and Problems, designed, in the hands of a good teacher, to arouse and strengthen in the student's mind the power of reasoning in accordance with sound scientific methods.

SEARLE'S OUTLINES OF ASTRONOMY. By AR-

THUR SEARLE, of Harvard College Observatory 1.60   2.00

This work is intended to give such elementary instruction in the principal branches of Astronomy as is required in High Schools or by any students not far advanced in mathematics. It is illustrated by carefully prepared engravings, and contains some information on each of the following subjects : —

1. The chief results of astronomical inquiry up to the present time with regard to the general constitution of the universe, and, in particular, with regard to the stars, planets, nebulæ, comets, and meteors.
2. The methods of astronomical research, and their application to the arts.
3. The general principles of theoretical astronomy.
4. The history of astronomy.
5. Astronomical statistics.

PRIMARY ARITHMETIC. By G. L. DEMAREST .   .40   .50

THE CHANDLER DRAWING-BOOK. By the late

JOHN S. WOODMAN, of Dartmouth College 80   1.00

THE NATIONAL MUSIC COURSE. In Four Books.

For Public Schools By JULIUS EICHBERG, J. B. SHARLAND, L. W. MASON, H. E. HOLT, Supervisors of Music in Public Schools of Boston, Mass.

PRIMARY OR FIRST MUSIC READER 24   .30
A course of exercises in the elements of VOCAL MUSIC AND SIGHT-SINGING, with choice rote songs for the use of youngest pupils.

INTERMEDIATE MUSIC READER 56   .70
Including the Second and Third Music Readers. A course of instruction in the elements of Vocal Music and Sight-Singing, with choice rote songs, in two and three parts, based on the elements of harmony.

THE FOURTH MUSIC READER. 8vo. pp. 336 $1.20 $1.50

This work, prepared to follow the Third Music Reader, is also adapted, under a competent instructor, to be used in High Schools where no previous systematic instruction has been given. To this end a brief but thorough elementary course is given, with musical theory, original solfeggios, a complete system of triad practice, and sacred music and song, with accompaniment for the piano. The music introduced is of a high order, and by the best masters, and is calculated to cultivate the taste, as well as to extend the knowledge and skill of the pupils.

THE FIFTH, or HIGH SCHOOL MUSIC READER

FOR MIXED VOICES. Containing a full Course of Advanced Solfeggios for One and Two Voices, and a carefully selected number of easy *Four*-Part Songs, taken from the works of the best composers. This work has been especially compiled to meet the growing wants of our High Schools for a higher grade of music than is contained in works now used in such schools.

N. B. — The Tenor Part in many of the songs may be either omitted or sung by the altos (boys).

THE ABRIDGED FOURTH MUSIC READER.
1.00   1.25

SECOND MUSIC READER   .   .   .   `.   .   .   .32   .40

THIRD MUSIC READER 32   .40

THE NATIONAL MUSIC CHARTS. By LUTHER

WHITING MASON. An invaluable aid to Teachers of Common Schools in imparting a practical knowledge of Music, and teaching Children to sing at sight. In Four Series. Forty Charts each. Price, $10.00 each Series.

FIRST SERIES 10.00
SECOND SERIES 10.00
THIRD SERIES 10.00
FOURTH SERIES, by L. W. MASON and J. B. SHARLAND 10.00
EASEL 1.25

THE NATIONAL MUSIC TEACHER. A Practical

Guide for Teaching Vocal Music to Young Children. By L. W. MASON   .   .   .60

GREEK.

GOODWIN'S GREEK GRAMMAR. By WILLIAM W.

GOODWIN, Ph. D., Eliot Professor of Greek Literature in Harvard University.
Half morocco $1.25 $1.56

The object of this Grammar is to state *general principles* clearly and distinctly, with special regard to those who are preparing for college. In the sections on the Moods are stated, for the first time in an elementary form, the principles which are elaborated in detail in the author's " Syntax of the Greek Moods and Tenses."

GREEK MOODS AND TENSES. The Fourth Edition.

By WILLIAM W. GOODWIN, Eliot Professor of Greek Literature in Harvard University. 1 vol. 12mo. Cloth. pp. 264 . . . . 1.40 1.75

This work was first published in 1860, and it appeared in a new form — much enlarged and in great part rewritten — in 1865. In the present edition the whole has been again revised; some sections and notes have been rewritten, and a few notes have been added. The object of the work is to give a plain statement of the princi ples which govern the construction of the Greek Moods and Tenses, — the most important and the most difficult part of Greek Syntax.

GOODWIN'S GREEK READER. Consisting of Extracts

from Xenophon, Plato, Herodotus, and Thucydides; being a full equivalent for the seven books of the Anabasis, now required for admission at Harvard. With Maps, Notes, References to GOODWIN'S GREEK GRAMMAR, and parallel References to CROSBY'S and HADLEY'S GRAMMARS. Edited by PROFESSOR W. W. GOODWIN, of Harvard College, and J. H. ALLEN, Cambridge. Half morocco 1.60 2.00

This book contains the third and fourth books of the Anabasis (entire), the greater part of the second book of the Hellenica, and the first chapter of the Memorabilia, of Xenophon; the last part of the Apology, and the beginning and end of the Phaedo, of Plato; selections from the sixth, seventh, and eighth books of Herodotus, and from the fourth book of Thucydides.

LEIGHTON'S GREEK LESSONS. Prepared to accompany

Goodwin's Greek Grammar. By R. F. LEIGHTON, Master of Melrose High School. Half morocco 1.25 1.56

This work contains about one hundred lessons, with a progressive series of exercises (both Greek and English), mainly selected from the first book of Xenophon's Anabasis. The exercises on the Moods are sufficient, it is believed, to develop the general principles as stated in the Grammar. The text of four chapters of the Anabasis is given entire, with notes and references. Full vocabularies accompany the book.

LIDDELL & SCOTT'S GREEK-ENGLISH LEXI-

CON. Abridged from the new Oxford Edition. New Edition. With Appendix of Proper and Geographical Names, by J. M. WHITON.
Morocco back 2 40 3.00
Sheep binding 2 80 3.50

LIDDELL & SCOTT'S GREEK-ENGLISH LEXI-

CON. The sixth Oxford Edition unabridged. 4to. Morocco back . . 9.60 12.00
Sheep binding . . 10.40 13.00

We have made arrangements with Messrs. Macmillan & Co. to publish in this country their new edition of Liddell & Scott's Greek Lexicons, and are ready to supply the trade.

The English editions of Liddell & Scott are *not stereotyped;* but each has been thoroughly revised, enlarged, and printed anew The sixth edition, just published, is larger by one eighth than the fifth, and contains 1865 pages. It is an *entirely different work* from the first edition, the whole department of etymology having been rewritten in the light of modern investigations, and the forms of the irregular verbs being given in greater detail by the aid of Veitch's Catalogue. No student of Greek can afford to dispense with this invaluable Lexicon, the price of which is now for the first time brought within the means of the great body of American scholars.

PLATO'S APOLOGY OF SOCRATES AND CRITO.
Edited, for the Use of Schools, by JOHN WILLIAMS WHITE, A. M.

The basis of this work will be the German edition of Dr Christian Cron. (Platons Vertheidigungsrede des Sokrates und Kriton. Fuenfte Auflage. Leipzig, Teubner, 1872.) To the matter contained in Dr. Cron's edition there will be added notes by the Editor and from other sources, analyses, and extended references to Goodwin and Hadley The book will be for the class-room, and all matter not of direct value to the student will be rigidly excluded.

THE ŒDIPUS TYRANNUS OF SOPHOCLES Edited, with an Introduction, Notes, and full explanation of the metres, by JOHN W. WHITE, A. M., Professor of the Greek Language and Literature in Baldwin University 1.20   1.50

THE MEDEA OF EURIPIDES. Edited, with Notes and an Introduction, by FREDERIC D. ALLEN, Ph. D., Professor in the University of Cincinnati.

WILKIN'S MANUAL OF GREEK PROSE COMPOSITION. 1 vol. 12mo. Cloth 2.00   2.50

WHITE'S FIRST LESSONS IN GREEK. Prepared to accompany Goodwin's Greek Grammar, and designed as an Introduction to his Greek Reader. By JOHN WILLIAMS WHITE, A. M., Tutor in Greek in Harvard College 1.00   1.25

A series of eighty lessons with progressive Greek-English and English-Greek exercises. Followed by selected passages from the first two books of Xenophon's Anabasis, and vocabularies.

WHITON'S SELECT ORATIONS OF LYSIAS. Comprising the Defence of Mantitheus, the Oration against Eratosthenes, the Reply to " The Overthrow of the Democracy," and the Oration on account of the Olive-Trunk ; with Introductions, Notes, and References to Goodwin's and Hadley's Greek Grammars, and Goodwin's Greek Moods and Tenses; adapted for use in Colleges, and in the highest classes of Academies. By JAMES MORRIS WHITON, Ph. D. 1.00   1.25

10907879R0

Made in the USA
Lexington, KY
28 August 2011